The English Jesuits
from
Campion to Martindale

The English Jesuits from Campion to Martindale

Bernard Basset, SJ
abridged and edited by Rodger Charles, SJ

GRACEWING

First published in 2004

Gracewing
2 Southern Avenue, Leominster
Herefordshire HR6 0QF

ISBN 0 85244 599 7

Typeset by Action Publishing Technology Ltd,
Gloucester GL1 5SR

Contents

Edmund Campion's address to the jury
after he and his companions had been condemned to death
1 December 1581

'Campion's voice rose in triumph.
He was no longer haggling with perjurers:
he spoke now for the whole gallant company
of the English Counter Reformation:
to all his contemporaries and all the posterity of his race:
"It was not our death that ever we feared.
But we knew that we were not lords of our own lives,
and therefore for want of answer, would not be guilty of our deaths.
The only thing we have to say now is,
that, if our religion do make us traitors,
we are worthy to be condemned, but otherwise are and have been,
as good servants as ever the Queen had.
In condemning us you are condemning all your own ancestors,
all the ancient priests, Bishops and Kings,
all that was once the glory of England, the Island of Saints,
and most devoted child of the See of Peter.
For what have we taught, however you may qualify it
with the odious name of treason, that they did not uniformly teach?
To be condemned by these lights, not of England only,
but of the whole world, is both gladness and glory to us.
God lives, posterity will live.
Their judgment is not so liable to corruption
as those who are about to condemn us to death."'

Evelyn Waugh, *Edmund Campion*, pp. 205–6

Preface

Terence Corrigan, SJ

History said Pope John XXII will be the guide to the Council. He meant that the movement of renewal in the Church could only be solid and genuine if it did not neglect the experience of the past. In the life of the Church we have to go back in order to go forward.

History is very important for any religious order when it engages in renewal urged by Vatican II since it is only through history that the 'true spirit of the founder' can be discovered. The founding of a religious order is always an attempt to live the life of the Gospel and to serve the needs of the Church in one's own day. After a time the institution can begin to run under its own momentum and in such a situation it is vitally important to look to the origins to discover the original inspiration. Fidelity is not routine. Jesuits for example cannot be defined by what they do since they do such different things, and Fr Basset's volume illustrates admirably the rich diversity of Jesuit life. The unity of Jesuits is to be sought in the special grace of St Ignatius; what Nadal called the *gratia capitalis*, the founder's grace. That is why at the 31st General Congregation of the Society of Jesus, historians were brought in from time to time to expound the mind of Ignatius on the topics under discussion. The appeal to the past was made to throw light on the problems of the present.

Fr Basset's book does not need a Provincial's preface. It

could go out into the world unprefaced, armed only with its own modestly worn learning and readability. I would like, though, to send it off with a blessing, not only because it is a magnificent story racily told, but because it reveals something important about what a Jesuit is, when the mists of myth have been blown away. Jesuits are not monks but the idea of community is as vital for the Jesuits as for any order of monks. Read Fr Basset's opening chapter and you will see the extraordinary importance attached to letter writing: it is a form of communication which keeps the bonds of charity alive, it enables superiors to know, sometimes with brutal frankness, what their men are thinking, it runs counter to eccentric individualism. The last General Congregation reaffirmed the importance today of community life. It noted that when it flourishes, the whole of religious life is sound. Obedience, for instance, is a very clear expression of our cooperation towards common ends, and it becomes more perfect to the extent that superiors and subjects are bound to one another in trust and service. Chastity is more safely preserved when there is true brotherly love in community between the members. The Jesuits of the English Province, scribbling their letters from prison, knew these things. Only where there is communication does charity become possible.

But a Jesuit community does not exist for its own sake. It is for the Church and people. That is why the actual work done can vary as needs change and new situations arise. History is not a matter of sighing over the past that is no more but a lesson in determining the signs of the times. That is why one lays down Fr Basset's book with the sense that now a new era is opening in the history of the Jesuits, in which the qualities of adaptation, patience, inventiveness, character and service will be needed. Those who actually heard Pope Paul's address to the Congregation cannot forget it. He told us that the Church accepts the promise of our work and the offer of our lives and since we are soldiers of Christ she calls us and entrusts to us difficult tasks in her name today more than ever. Fr Basset's necessary book will underline the need for community between the spirit of the past and the tasks of the future.

Terence Corrigan, SJ, Provincial
London, September 1967

Foreword

It has long been the custom in religious communities to
honour the memory of the dead. Obituary lists were care-
fully complied, to which were added biographical
sketches and such Menologies were read aloud at the
evening meal. Recently at Lanherne I learned how Sister
Joseph Mary, summoned by the Superior, was so prompt
in her obedience that she left a kettle of scalding water on
the stairs. Sister had three brothers who were Jesuits but I
doubt if they carried perfection as far as this. The practice
of reading aloud the merits of former brethren is salutary.
At worst such biographies are good for a laugh; at best
they issue a challenge, for the pattern of true holiness
cannot be obscured by passing fashion and the Eternal
remains ever fresh. The English Jesuits dutifully revised
their Menology at intervals, the last revision being done
over a century ago by Fr John Macleod, a scholar with a
mild bias towards the Scottish aristocracy. A frivolous [xi]
obituary reproduced the spirit in which Macleod
presented his subjects. The Jesuit in question was said to
have completed his studies at Ghent, and most likely was
sent to England. Of his death there's no trace as to time or
to place. He was a Scot and of noble descent.

A Canadian superior of undoubted charm persuaded
me to accept this present undertaking; in so doing he [xii]
unwittingly invited one of his subjects to enter a field in

which angels fear to tread. Omissions I make may annoy some Jesuits, secular priests may be put off by too many threadbare controversies, while experts may point out that I have not read this or that. After three years of solid reading I remain an amateur. Oxford trained, I have clung to the advice of Mr David Ogg, my illustrious tutor, to read and read until you know the subject and then write. This I have done. It is a thrilling story. In writing it I have had access to Stonyhurst and English Province archives and have relied where possible on printed sources. I believe that I have told an honest tale and am proud to have read as as much anti-Jesuit as pro-Jesuit literature. Indeed, when I began my work I was not particularly Jesuit-minded and remain in a delicate balance at the end.

I had help from many and they are all commendably shy. My Superiors let me get on with it and never [xv] interfered. I have been given kindness and trust from Jesuits and non-Jesuits alike. I had the early assistance of two Jesuit experts: Fr Leo Hicks, SJ and Herbert Chadwick, SJ. Anxious about many finer points, I know I have told an honest story and am pleased to assert that every view I have expressed is my own. I do not regret the considerable labour. I owe a massive debt to the Society of Jesus after forty years. Sister Mary Joseph, at the start of this foreword, foolishly left a kettle of scalding water on the stairs. Still more foolishly, I have picked it up.

Introduction

Rodger Charles, SJ

The Catholic Bourbon monarchs were bitter enemies of the Papacy. The Jesuits were its staunchest defenders. Get rid of them and the Papacy could be dealt with. It is a bitter irony that the Bourbon monarch's influence in the conclave of 1769 meant that a Pope could be elected who might be pressured into suppressing the Society. One was, and Clement XIV did their bidding with the brief *Dominus ac Redemptor* which took effect on 16 August 1773. By a remarkable series of coincidences the Society survived and in 1803 there was a partial restoration which applied to the English Province and in 1814 the Society was fully restored. We are now celebrating the two-hundredth anniversary of that restoration, and this abridgment of Basset's volume is one Jesuit's contribution to that celebration. That volume tells us how the traditions of the English Province developed before the suppression, how it recovered after it and what great work it did thereafter. As Fr Corrigan's preface says, it is a magnificent story, racily told, as I hope the bare bones I have revealed show. It is also a work of scholarship, dealing with complex issues of Church and State, of social and political change over more than four hundred years, and of gradual read-mission to the mainstream of national life from the early nineteenth century.

In abridging, one tries to make accessible the essentials

of what an author says by selecting from his text those sentences or passages which are central to his reasoning and conclusions, but leaving out those passages which, for example, quote copiously from original sources, or deal in detail with objections to his thesis, or on the other hand quote others in his favour. These are necessary to the scholar, but not to those who only wish to understand the basic message. The purpose of this work then is to make accessible the essentials of the book as it was published in 1967. Of course aspects of his historical and other judgements are now dated because of more recent research, yet the work is still a classic, and from the point of view of this celebration it has lost none of its value.

There are problems in abridging when, for example, one passage of the author's text, when placed with another such passage, reads badly because of repetitions of the same words or because reference is made to facts elided in the abridgement. In places it has been necessary to add or subtract a word here or there, but they are few. The text is literally almost one hundred per cent Basset's. In that text I have given, for easy reference, the number of each page (in square brackets) of the original which was abridged. I hope this encourages the readers who are further interested, to become familiar with that original.

Fr Bernard Basset was one of a group of Jesuits who particularly inspired us with fervour for the mission in the rather somnolent years before the Council, and his book captures the spiritual élan of our predecessors in their days of glory AMDG. The mission and Province grew out of the primitive inspiration of the Order. Ignatius placed his men at the disposal of the papacy and the teaching Church; English Jesuits, in Garnet's words, were guilty of no treason other than upholding orthodox Catholic doctrines. As Basset puts it, they accepted outright the Roman attitude. Thinking with the Church meant thinking with the Pope.

Garnet died for the faith, and we honour him for that, while we thank God that the conflict between Christians that was part of our past has been replaced by mutual love and respect, and we look forward to the day when we can be one again. Respect for the martyrs, of all traditions, should not conflict with these hopes. As Pope Paul VI said, on the occasion of the canonization of the forty English Catholic martyrs in 1970, this event should not open old wounds, but give us an opportunity to recognize our faults and ask pardon for them. We should see in the martyrs a shining example of that genuine faith that is never afraid to declare its convictions. From 1580 the General, Everard Mercurian, sent Jesuits to England at Cardinal Allen's request. Lord Salisbury saw in them the main threat to a lasting Protestant settlement so he manipulated the law to make it appear they were entirely responsible for the dubious Gunpowder Plot [1605]. They were not: but the national myth of the seditious Jesuit was established. Lord Shaftesbury exploited it for two years at the time of the fictitious Popish Plot [1678]. The blood lust was kept alive by the Whigs. James II's imprudence lead to the loss of his crown in 1688, leaving the Catholic community much weakened and the Jesuits particularly at risk.

Meanwhile the whole Society was officially surpressed for forty years. It was restored 1803–14 and when English Catholics were free to practise their faith once more in 1829, English Jesuits did their part in helping rebuild the Church in their homeland. By the early twentieth century, as our author so neatly puts it below, a Jesuit could call in at Buckingham Palace, to sip a cup of Imperial tea.

1

Jesuit correspondence

Jesuits learned from their founder to be letter writers: his
run to nine thousand pages of print. Most were on matters [1]
of immediate practical import. Superiors at every level
and throughout the world had obligations of sending
reports to their own superiors; such official correspondence could, and did, show personal concerns for their
subjects, the health of this man, the wandering proclivities
of another. All aspects of the mission had to be on record.
Each Jesuit has the right of direct access by letter to the
General on matters of urgent business or simply personal
requests or desire for information. Individual Jesuits
wrote frequently to one another, revealing deeper [2]
emotions than normally allowed to them in history books.
Campion's letters to his friends in Bohemia on his way to
his death in England give the sober, deeply spiritual side.
Those between Frs John Thorpe in Rome, Charles Plowden
at Lulworth in Dorset and John Carroll in Washington, at
the end of the eighteenth century, are less serious and
more colourful matters. The *Annual Letters* compiled by
superiors from notes submitted by their subjects were
important. Naive and unselfconscious, they throw a
refreshing light on Jesuit undertakings and form a rich
seam of history, linking contrasting experiences of different men, problems and regions. The Generals for example [3]
were concerned that their subjects in England, harried as

they were by their persecutors, seemed at times neglectful of them and were gently chided for this; information for the *Annual Letters*, was even more important from them. Acquaviva reminded them of their duty to make sure the virtues of their men were recorded, for the information of those who come after. It was what they themselves knew or had heard from creditable sources which Rome wanted to know. So Persons wrote a factual account of Campion's experiences, and John Gerard's biography was the result of similar prompting.

Rome however did not always appreciate how difficult it was to get information through. For two centuries and more recusants were hesitant to use the public mails

[4] because they were routinely searched. Eventually friendly ambassadors could oblige; so could Catholics travelling on the continent. The result was that letters could take two months to get to Rome and replies could take six to get to

[5] England. Jesuit archives existed but were always at risk. That many were preserved was due to Fr Christopher Grene, an Irishman who joined the Society in 1658. He lived mainly in Italy, but working with his brother Martin,

[6] a Jesuit in England was able to save stacks of documents on Jesuit affairs.

John Gerard's *Autobiography* was smuggled out of Rome

[7] at this time. Few other documents can rival his in story, length, style and character, but there were many shorter narratives, as exciting and as observant. The Jesuits were educated men, always in danger, often hiding, yet burrowing in every county and in daily contact with Englishmen of every type. Theirs was an experience quite beyond the range of court diarists like Pepys. Then outside England English Jesuits travelled widely; Andrew White to Maryland, Thomas Stevens to India, John Yates to Brazil. The majority of Jesuits wrote only for other Jesuits, without a trace of special pleading or an eye to the

[8] centuries ahead. But for the efforts of Henry Foley, a Victorian Jesuit, few of these accounts would have been known or read.

Foley's father was vicar of a Worcestershire parish. Henry was articled to a local solicitor, eventually settling down as a lawyer and marrying. In 1846 he was received into the Church in Worcester and when his wife died in 1851 he, at forty, joined the Society. He did not feel called to the priesthood, and given his legal experience he, as a brother, gave invaluable service as secretary to several Provincials. In this work he came to read the Province papers and his virtues of industry and integrity enabled him to produce the *Records of the English Province SJ* whose volumes, eight thousand pages in all, appeared 1877–1883. For them he gutted the Stonyhurst archives as well as collecting documents from elsewhere, in fact most of the other material available. The work has its imperfections but among reputable historians, many of whom rely on his material, his name stands high. George Oliver published [9] biographies of Scottish, English and Irish Jesuits. *Annual Letters* was replaced in 1863 by *Letters and Notices*, a series [10] which still goes on. Much of their matter is ephemeral, but there is much that is genuine historical record.

In these resources there is a unique record of Englishmen who came in 1580, unwanted and invited, and despite three hundred years of active persecution, they never left. It would be difficult to find in English history [11] any comparable group, universally derided for so many centuries. They survived the first century of active, bitter persecution, a second century in which they were isolated and ignored. They were attacked most bitterly by a number of fellow Roman Catholics, and for forty years were officially suppressed. Yet in 1829, when Catholic Emancipation gave room for modest expansion the Jesuits were ready, with an enthusiasm unquenched by two centuries and more of unrelenting hostility, to respond to the needs of the Church. Indeed their Victorian expansion followed arrangements drawn up in 1619. They entered England fit only for the gallows and lived to see Fr Bernard Vaughan, by the early twentieth century, call in at Buckingham Palace to sip a cup of Imperial tea.

Newman in his Anglican days wrote a letter which Victorian Jesuits were glad to preserve. The letter confesses that the atrocious lies – he can call them nothing else – which were circulated against him led him to to feel how very false the popular impression may be about the [12] Jesuits.

2

The first recruits

Ignatius, as an impoverished student in Paris, came to England in 1530 in order the' beg alms from Spanish merchants in London. As General he was on good terms [13] with the exiled Cardinal Pole, but by the time the Society came to be, England and the papacy were sundered. Mary Tudor (1553–1558) tried to restore the Catholic Church of her youth but failed. The older Orders returned, but only one Jesuit came on Spanish business and did not stay. By the time of his death in 1556 Ignatius' order had but one English and one Irish member. Thomas Lith became a Jesuit lay brother in 1557 and served as cook in Rome and infirmarian in Lithuania, being highly praised for his work there. With the coming of Elizabeth (1558–1603) many Catholics, mainly from the universities, were forced to flee abroad. In their exile they met a booming Society of Jesus which had expanded to 3,500 members within twenty-five years. Many were attracted to it, mainly because it was a religious order and because it was modern. It had shed many old customs but it had a community life and its religious practices. It also had a singleness of purpose and a strong appeal because of its missionary work; Francis Xavier's exploits were the talk of Catholic Europe. Some of the first Marian exiles who joined the Order had held high preferment. Some were distinguished academics. William [15] Good had been a canon of Wells, Thomas Derbyshire

Chancellor of the London Diocese, the Heywood brothers, Fellows of All Souls. The latter were great nephews of Thomas More, as probably also was John Rastall. Adam Brooke, Thomas Langdale and George Ware also entered the Society at this time.

Ignatius stipulated that those who applied to join should be men not boys, and that health was more important than wealth or status; class distinctions were ignored. Practical judgement, prudence and aptitude for work rather than sharpness of intellect were the criteria; the sort of things that would determine success had the applicant [16] chosen to stay in the secular world. Ignatius thought personal appearance was important. Spiritually, morally and intellectually all these early candidates were well qualified. They could not hope to return to England. They went to work in the European universities: Rome, Paris, Louvain, Triers and others. They taught philosophy, theology, Latin, Greek and Hebrew. Three Englishmen still in [17] prison at home applied to join. Thomas Woodhouse was a Marian priest who probably took his vows before being hanged in 1571. Thomas Mettam, also a priest, a Doctor of Divinity, and a friend of Fr Derbyshire, took his vows in 1579, and remained in prison for seventeen years at Wisbech. He was much respected by his fellow prisoners. The disputes at Wisbech after his death reveal how his presence had calmed things. Thomas Pounde, a layman, spent some thirty years in jail. A wealthy aristocrat who once cut a dazzling figure at Elizabeth's court, he had been attracted to the Society by Xavier's work and gathered other young men with the intention of going to the Indian mission. Thomas Stevens eventually got there: Pounde was arrested the night he was to sail. The General allowed [18] him to take his vows in jail, probably in 1578.

A second wave of volunteers applied in the 1570s, mainly from universities. Brought up in Mary's reign, and at university under the Elizabethan settlement, some of them being Anglicans, many had been deeply disturbed and were confused as a result. Some of the younger ones

wanted, when ordained, to return to England, others just
wished to study in peace. Few of them had heard of the
Society: all knew of Dr Allen's seminary at Douai. It was
to Douai that the exiled Catholic dons of the 1560s had
rallied. Save for a short break at Rheims, the College
would be at Douai until the French revolutionary wars. It [19]
was unique, a seminary in which was fostered in young
men a spirit of devotion rarely equalled before or since.
Priests and future priests who wanted to return to
England went first to Douai and many joined the Society
eventually. Before 1580 they included Briant, Cottam,
Cornelius, Southwell, Campion, Holt, Holtby, Currie and
Bennett. Allen's plan to send priests back into England did
not please everyone; many thought it too bold and revolutionary; some wanted to practise as priests on the
Continent. Many who admired Allen's work had become
so restless that they wanted to move on.

Campion's case reflected the confusion. The son of a
London bookseller, Edmund's academic gifts opened the
path to Oxford for him by his scholarship. His career as an
undergraduate and young don at St Johns was brilliant
indeed; he was the idol of his generation and a favourite of
the Earl of Leicester. He eventually went to Douai in 1570
and was welcomed by Gregory Martin, a good friend who
had made his choice earlier. Edmund was very happy
there but in 1572 went to Rome and applied to join the
Jesuit noviceship, being welcomed with open arms, and
allotted to the Austrian Province. He did his noviceship at [20]
Brunn, and was happy there. After struggles with scruples, hesitation and doubt, the peace and security of
religious life was to his taste. Few at the time realized that
men as sane as he found peace and purpose in religious
life. To his lasting credit, and against his own immediate
interests, Allen was one of the few who did.

Robert Persons, Fellow and Bursar at Balliol College in
Oxford had, like Campion, taken the Anglican oath with
misgivings. He had consulted with Campion in Oxford
and the news of his becoming a Jesuit affected him. He

was soon to leave Oxford himself, some said because because of immorality and theft, which still leaves us free to accept Persons' own version, that it was for conscience sake he resigned. At his departure some comedian pealed the College bells.

Persons has a sinister reputation, but on closer acquaintance he proves to be amusing and lovable. In writing of Campion he is affectionate and respectful whereas he makes no attempt to make himself appear edifying. When he fled to Calais he did not have priesthood in mind but with John Yates, an Oxford friend, he planned to study [21] medicine in Padua. In Flanders however he did the Spiritual Exercises of St Ignatius which gave him a nudge to enter religious life but nothing came of it and so he travelled comfortably to Rome and then Padua, retiring briefly to a monastery, intending to stay there, which he did not. He returned to Rome and eventually entered the noviceship at St Andrea in July 1575.

Fr William Good, who gave the exercises to Persons in Flanders, was one of the two or three Jesuits who played a [22] part in bringing the Jesuits to England. All the other Marian priests were teaching on the Continent; Bosgrove at Olmuz and Vilna, one of the Heywoods at Antwerp, the other at Dillingen. Good had a roving commission, held many responsible posts and had the knack of being unexpectedly at the right places at the right times. Born in Glastonbury, he was a Fellow of Corpus Christi College Oxford and had high preferment in Somerset under Mary. Fleeing to Flanders in 1562 he joined the Society at Tournai, where Everard Mercurian, future General, was his Provincial. As General, Mercurian sent him on a mission to Ireland, accompanying the future Archbishop of Armagh. He was back in Louvain in time to give Persons and John Yates the Exercises, so changing their lives. Persons kept in touch with Good. [23] Yates went to Brazil as a Jesuit, from where he would pen a glowing tribute to his friend when he heard news of his death in 1586.

Good was friendly with the General and Dr Allen as

well as Persons. In 1577 he was sent on a mission to Sweden. He returned to Rome after two years and his name was mentioned when the Jesuit mission to England in 1580 was under discussion but it was decided he was too old to join it. He died in 1586. Thomas Derbyshire was [23] another who had great influence on the history of the mission. Born 1518, he was probably a student at Broadgate Hall (now Pembroke College) Oxford in 1535. Derbyshire became rector of Hackney in 1554, then Archdeacon of Essex and rector of the Church of St Magnus London Bridge and Chancellor of the Diocese of London. He was imprisoned on the accession of Elizabeth. [24] Exiled, he thought of becoming a Carthusian, but entered the Society in 1563. He acted as rector of a College while he was a novice and, in 1556 probably, went to Scotland on papal business, then professed Theology at Dillingen and for a while was novice master at Billom in France. In Paris as honorary agent for English affairs, Derbyshire lectured publicly with great success. Yet it was his social skills and his ability to gain the confidence of young people which proved a decisive factor in Jesuit history. Robert Southwell, brilliant but unhappy, was successfully counselled by him. Richard Holtby, a seminary priest from Yorkshire, [25] rode to London, sold his horse to pay his fare to visit him, made the Exercises with him, and entered the noviciate at Verdun.

John Currie, another seminary priest from England, came to see him with the same results. Henry Fitzsimon, an Irish Protestant who was in Europe to defeat the Papists, met his match in Fr Derbyshire, and returned to Ireland a Jesuit to endure years of hardship and persecution in the bogs outside Waterford. The seventeen-year-old John Gerard, travelling on the Continent, was already much intrigued by Jesuits and when taken ill in Paris, was helped by Derbyshire. They travelled together to Rouen to meet Persons and thus it was that one of the most remarkable of English Jesuits was honourably ensnared. George Gilbert, a rich young man on tour in Europe, arrived in

Paris in 1577, having already cut a dash at the French Court, and met Derbyshire socially and on friendly terms [25] as a fellow Englishman. Gilbert revealed he had severe difficulties with the doctrine of assurance of salvation of the Puritan sect to which he belonged. Outgoing and highly successful he, as so many others of the time, was not sure of his state of soul. Gilbert was impressed by Derbyshire's answers, but still more by the example of his life. He was convinced, and left Paris for Rome determined on a pilgrimage to the Holy Land. In Rome he met Persons, just ordained, and was reconciled to the Church by him; he also persuaded him to return to England to prepare for the arrival of the seminary priests. Gilbert, in practical terms, was the true founder of the Jesuit English [26] mission. Between them Good and Derbyshire fashioned the mission of the English Jesuits. Persons, Yates, Southwell, Currie, Holtby, Gerard, Lane, Fitzimmons and Gilbert owed their vocations as Jesuits to them. Like Good, Derbyshire was considered for the 1580 mission but was discarded as too old. In fact he lived on into his eighties, dying in 1604, full well contented to use Persons' phrase.

3

The Jesuit invasion

Only Dr Allen could supply the ingenuity which was
needed to get the Jesuits to come to England. There was a [27]
mutual respect between them. They admired the other's
qualities and borrowed ideas and method from one
another. The English students received much help from
Flemish Jesuits and Allen numbered the General, Mercurian and Fr Derbyshire among his friends. Allen was
English to the core, a Lancashire man from Rossall,
medieval in his politics but far ahead of his time as an
educator. He saw Elizabeth as a usurper and disliked her,
and thought that given a choice the English people would
desert her, and so had no difficulty with Spanish or papal
forces aiding the process. He and his exiled friends had for
nineteen years down to 1580 been plotting how to bring
this about. For this reason they saw Pius V's excommuni-
cation of the Queen in 1570 as a step in the right direction. [28]
Imposing the faith by force was not his plan. He simply
wanted to help the English people restore that faith of
which they had been deprived by force. Unlike the exiles
in general however, his motives were entirely spiritual:
Catholicism in England would die without priests. Douai
was opened to train them and in 1577 fifty young Englishmen arrived for the purpose. Seventeen had already been
ordained and returned to England, and twenty more were
ready to sail. The possibility of marytrdom was there, but

remotely. Cuthbert Mayne's execution at Launceston in
[29] 1577 was an exceptional case. The young priests were
receiving a warm welcome from their fellow Catholics,
confirming to Allen that his countrymen would return to
the faith given a chance. For many years his diagnosis may
have been correct. Only gradually did it become plain it
was not.

The seminary at Rheims was overcrowded and short of
[29] funds. Allen was seeking to get the English hospice in
Rome to take the overflow, and at the same time in 1577 he
sought to get help from the Jesuits on the mission, since
young Englishmen were joining them in numbers, and
though this was discussed with enthusiasm by some, the
General was hesitant. He had allowed Persons and
Derbyshire to keep the twenty-four English Jesuits in
Rome together but none were going to England. The
Society was already overcommitted to other parts of the
[30] world. Mercurian had been shocked by the way some
British ecclesiastics at the hospice in Rome were behaving.
These problems concerned the clash between English and
Welsh interests, but there was also disagreement over
Allen's policies; not all were possessed with his burning
[31] enthusiasm over the mission.

It was at Allen's request, and much against the inclina-
tion of superiors, as Persons tells us, that the General
loaned the mission two Italian Jesuits who worked with
the Welsh Rector of the English College. Their position
was unenviable, but they gradually won the affection of
many of the students who then began to insist that the
Jesuits took over its running. Inevitably the charge was
[32] made that they had fostered the discontents to get control.
Whether they did or not we have no way of knowing but
Persons and Derbyshire were angered and Mercurian
thought of withdrawing his men. Persons was now
consulted by a group of the students and became a close
friend of one of the leaders, young Ralph Sherwin, who
was to die with Campion at Tyburn. Persons' ability to
influence such young men and gain their confidence

showed his extraordinary sympathy with them. Until this time he had been, since leaving Oxford, a fish out of water. Through these seminarians in Rome he found his cause; total identification with Allen and his mission. He told the General that some English Jesuits were willing to shed their blood there and he was one. Finally the Pope ordered the General to take charge of the College.

Allen came to Rome in 1579 to restore peace and help [33] with organization, and the question of the Jesuit mission to England came up once more. It was hardly possible, it was said, for Jesuits to train men for its dangers without their readiness to share the risks. The reputation of the Society, its apologetic skills, its freedom from entanglements with church lands which so harassed the older orders, were all advanced as reasons why they should. It was also pointed out that more Englishmen had joined the Society than any other order. These arguments seem incomprehensible today. How Jesuits could be thought to be acceptable in England because of them it is hard to see. Mercurian, friend of Allen's though he was, was not impressed; he thought the Jesuit return would make things worse. Philip Hughes praises his practical wisdom and good judgement – the ability to deliberate calmly [34] about the good and the expedient. He saw first that the mission would be dismissed as political, that it would it very difficult for the priests to keep their rule in the irregular, hunted life they would lead, and it was wrong for men who had sacrificed so much in going to exile, to be sent back. Finally with no bishops in England, harmony among priests could hardly be expected.

Dr Allen prevailed, and we will judge that sadly or happily according to prejudice or convictions. There was joy among the English Jesuits in Rome and great hope that they might be selected to return to their homeland. Persons was surprised to be appointed as Superior, but it is a tribute to his integrity that he was. Allen's letter to Campion in December 1579 said that workaday priests were now not enough; what was needed was outstanding

missionaries with Campion at their head – an argument
[35] often resented later. Christopher Perkins in Germany
received a similar invitation and accepted it provided he
could take the oath of allegiance and attend non-Catholic
services. The documents of the period suggest that the
mission was seen as a delicate rather than a dangerous
one.

Campion had been teaching in Prague since his noviceship ended and he was now thirty-nine. He was Professor
of Rhetoric in the Jesuit College, writing and producing
plays, which amused him greatly. He corresponded with
Persons, Bavant his former tutor, and with Gregory
Martin, but the letters are marked by his genuine absorp-
tion with his pupils. In one to Persons in Rome he remarks
casually that he was willing to return to England should
God will it, but otherwise he was very contented in
Prague. When told of the execution of Cuthbert Mayne, his
[36] old pupil, his genuine admiration for him implied no great
desire to go to England. Allen's letter dated 9th December
told him that the General had decided he should go. When
confirmation arrived two months later, he set out at once,
leaving part of his heart in Bohemia.

The Jesuit invasion was in truth ill prepared and so
miscalculated at every stage that it is a wonder that the
efficient Persons had anything to do with it. The English
Government knew about it before it left Rome. Persons,
Campion and Br Ralph Emerson were the only Jesuits of
the fourteen-strong party; preparations had been made in
a hurry and badly at that. Campion, the key figure, was
barely consulted and arrived at the last minute, tired, sick
[37] and ill informed. He had come from Bohemia by coach to
Innsbruck but walked his way to Padua. After eight days
in Rome he set out for the second time to walk across
Europe. His composure was remarkable. The organizers in
Rome were optimistic; they expected the reconversion of
the English people. Campion, however, knew they were
hopelessly out of touch with the realities in England;
he also knew he would die. Every day, after early Mass he

would walk a mile ahead, say his breviary, meditate and say the litany of the saints. An hour before lunch he rejoined his colleagues and was merry with them, talking the while of suffering for Christ. He preached when asked – with conviction and fire, but private conversation some-times revealed melancholy. Meeting his old friend Allen at Rheims he spoke as if he doubted the enterprise, on which he had embarked as a result of the Cardinal's efforts. The response was that his talents were needed, at which Campion declared himself ready to do as God willed. [38]

The confusion on the Channel coast confirmed Campion's realism because they discovered notices of their arrival had been posted at English ports. That there [39] had been another ill-judged armed expedition to Ireland did nothing to calm fears. Understandably the old Bishop of St Asaph who was with them decided that physically he was not up up to the crossing. In nothing is the muddled thinking that lay behind the expedition better exposed. That he was ever considered as fit for it is astonishing. Two more Jesuits joined them as they waited on the coast. Bosgrave, who had left his native country as a child, was returning for health reasons, his English rusty and knowing little of the Elizabethan settlement. The other man Thomas Cottam, who had a mind to go to India, joined the Roman noviceship for that purpose, but caught a fever which Roman doctors said required recuperation in his native air. When he landed in Dover in 1580, he was immediately arrested, betrayed by a false friend he had met en route. [40]

Good sense was now shown by the party as they approached England by different routes, going variously via Dieppe, Rouen, Boulogne and Dunkirk. Here the three original Jesuit members of the party were for the first time their own masters. They went to the Walloon Jesuits at St Omers who did not think it a good idea they should go on since the English government was expecting them. Persons, the Superior, thought otherwise. He decided that since they had been told to go, boldness might be the best policy. Had his plan gone wrong and he had ended at Tyburn he would have been celebrated for his courage and other virtues, as was Campion. Mercurian had given them a list of simple and prudent rules. He had no knowledge of what conditions they would find, but he wanted them to be on their guard. They must make clear their mission was spiritual, to confirm Catholics in their faith, not to contest with heretics. They were to avoid politics and never mention the Queen. To avoid misunderstandings they should only consort with men, and avoid giving the impression they were legacy hunters in the high society in which they would have to mix; care of souls was their concern alone.

Community life would be difficult, so in its absence [41] they were to visit each other frequently. Soutanes were for services in secret only. Lay dress should be modest. For disguise Campion called himself Mr Edmonds. Persons eventually had ten aliases. The need for Jesuits to have [42] them lasted until 1850. Persons, the first Jesuit to invade England, chose to travel as an officer returning from the [43] Netherlands, and dressed to look the part. At Dover he chatted with officials and hired a horse from one of them; he even told them that his friend Mr Edmonds, a diamond merchant, would be coming through shortly. In London in the early morning he felt conspicuous in the deserted streets. Ever resourceful, he crossed to Southwark knowing he could make contact with jailed Catholics there. In the Marshalsea he met Thomas Pounde himself. Breakfasting there, he was then taken to George Gilbert's house in Fetter Lane. Campion followed later. He could not emulate Persons' aplomb but he ended up with Gilbert, and details how the young men were on hand to re-apparel, furnish him and weapon him and ride with him out of the city. He visited different parts each day and [44] found the harvest great.

George Gilbert and his friends Brinckly, Vaux, Basset, Fitzherbert and the rest won the undying admiration and love of the priests they helped. Persons referred to

Gilbert, not Campion or Allen, as his closest friend. Without them one can wonder whether the missioners would have lasted a week. It was Persons who had reconciled Gilbert to the church, and who dissuaded him from the pilgrimage to the Holy Land in order to look after the priests. He had become engaged in the meantime, but once the priests arrived he abandoned his beloved for the length of the Jesuits' stay. Gilbert supported them and [45] looked to their safety himself, supplied their clothing, horses and finance and all very generously. He wanted the Fathers to be free for their ministry without depending on those ministered to. All Persons' schemes were financed by him and he always travelled with him. He prepared their missionary journeys and planned alternative escape routes. Few surpassed in him in the use of arms, in horsemanship or bodily agility and dexterity. He set down on paper the methods of Campion and Persons' day and he plays down his own part but shrewd writers and judges of men saw his association as a rudimentary lay religious order or Jesuit sodality. The organization seems to have been spontaneous, the result of a deep craving for the old religion by young and wealthy upper class men. Such [46] devotion led Persons and Allen to believe in ultimate success.

Gilbert and his friends were looking for leadership and this Campion, and still more Persons, could provide. Campion drew and held crowds with charm, learning and reputation. Persons was a born leader, his courage, eye for detail and an astonishing capacity for friendship made him a natural. Gilbert and his companions were Persons' men, planning books, manning and providing the presses with stocks of paper, distributing his pamphlets at night, in heretical houses, workshops, palaces, in court and in the streets. They put Persons in touch with the most devoted English families who would support the Jesuit mission for a century. Eventually this would cause resentment. In the first hectic year all were too busy to notice; the bond formed under fire was strong.

[47] Their relations with the clergy already in England were cooler. On their arrival the Jesuits went to St Mary's Southwark to explain themselves to senior priests. The likely charges of politics and treason against them were discussed, as was Trent's ruling about attendance at heretical services, and the more lenient fasting rules. Few Marian priests knew what the Jesuits were on; friction was less religious/secular, more Marian/seminary priests. The former had established a kind of peaceful co-existence over twenty years. The arrival of Campion and Sherwin was seen as unfortunate. All the topics were loaded; chances of dispensation for attending non-Catholic services, the purpose of Dr Sanders' expedition to Ireland, the effect of the Jesuit crusade. Mercurian had foreseen most of it. One grave old priest suggested the Jesuits go back and await the rosy dawn. Persons could only say that unless his orders were changed he must stay. He denied any knowledge of Sanders' Irish mission and showed Mercurian's instructions to avoid politics. One compromise was reached. The new laws on fasting would be accepted in theory but unhurriedly. Persons said the meeting ended with expressions of mutual affection and the grave and ancient priest said he was satisfied.

[48] After Southwark the Jesuits would be aware of a certain touchiness in the Marian clergy; Persons on the other hand could identify himself with the seminary priests. With Campion so often out of London in the first year he was reliant entirely on them, and he marvelled at their courage and cheerfulness, their readiness to help him in all things: Blackwell in writing his pamphlets, and Hartley supervising his secret press. They helped Gilbert's men with the distribution of the books and they saw personally that they got into the right hands whatever the risk. Brought to London they were distributed in parcels of 100 or 50, and they were issued simultaneously through the country. In letters to Rome Campion and Persons were rightly high in their praise of these young men, who embarrassingly, despite their virtue and learning, treated the Jesuits with

the greatest respect. This made them stress that any other [49]
Jesuits sent must be the very best, and that they needed the
prayers of all, that they do not fail the high expectations
placed in them. Given the mood of 1580 all this was no
more than the truth but it would cause offence later.

Campion and Persons asked for Spanish, Italian and
English priests. Since the penal laws, while strict, were not
yet tyrannical, they thought they could ride out the storm.
The foreign priests could live safely and deal with moral
and theological problems. Surprisingly, they asked for
Jasper Heywood, a middle-aged and cantankerous Professor of Hebrew who was subject to gout, as a recruit to the
mission. He had in his favour academic successes: he had [50]
also once been a page at Court and apparently in his youth
had known the Princess Elizabeth. He was much respected
in Bavaria and the Pope had to write to the Elector to get
his release. What Persons' apprehensions were in the first
few months we cannot be sure. Campion knew he would
be taken. He tells that he read news of himself wherever he
went, even that he had already been captured, and this so
overwhelmed him with fear, that its power made him fear-
less. Government pressure grew; Sherwin and Briant were
taken and George Gilbert was himself forced to flee.
Persons ordered him to go because government agents
were on his trail and he thought it foolish for his patron to
risk arrest. Typically he took much money with him before
going. He generously rescued a community of starving
nuns at Rouen and he was likewise open-handed to a
seminary at Rheims. He lived at the English College in
Rome, hoping to be of use to his fellow countrymen.

One thing remained to be done before the mission
collapsed. Campion was writing his *Ten Reasons*, going to [51]
ground in the north at Easter 1581, sheltered among others
by a seminary priest, Richard Holtby. The finished document was sent to Persons in London and thoroughly
checked by one of Gilbert's colleagues so that any mistakes
made in references were eliminated. Persons joined
Campion at Stonor Park near Oxford for the printing; the

press had been taken there for safety. They discussed what should be done if they were taken – as Campion soon was. Not daring to go into Henley once he knew Campion was in custody, Persons sent his man to report; he noted the tranquillity of the prisoner as the cavalcade rode off to London; his arms pinioned and a notice pinned to his hat saying Edmund Campion seditious Jesuit. Campion and Persons never met again.

A final incident in Campion's career deserves mention because it changed the whole aspect of the mission. The Jesuits had arrived in England in June 1580 and with London emptying because of the holiday season, both security and apostolic reasons dictated that they visited the provinces. They split into two parties of two and agreed to meet at Hoxton, so that Campion and Persons could renew their religious vows. Thomas Pounde, meanwhile had bribed his jailer so he could meet them there for the express purpose of getting them to put something on paper so that if one or both should be taken it could be publicized, and so [52] undermine any government attempt to spread disinformation. They were having a meal together when Pounde appeared and made his request. Persons agreed immediately but did nothing at once. Campion was less happy to agree, but being persuaded, immediately got up, found a quiet corner and there in half an hour dashed off what he would like to see published after his arrest.

He gave Pounde a copy unsealed and kept the original himself; the document came to be known as *Campion's Brag*. It had been the understanding that it should be confidential, but Pounde's ardent indiscretion, once he had read it, meant it was not. It was copied and passed from [53] hand to hand, causing anger or joy as it did so, and was on the table of the Privy Council in November. In it Campion demanded leave to debate with the University dons the religious questions. This was a challenge the Tudors had not faced in nearly a hundred years. He was not a prudent man. He had preached to a large congregation in Smithfield soon after arriving in London and a year later at

Lyford Grange he was to go back for a second night there, because he was asked to, and that lead to his capture. So here at Hoxton he dashed off a challenge as though he was composing the *Marseillaise*.

It proves a wise and most moving appeal. Its style, its thought, the very circumstances of its composition all add to its nobility. No Jesuit but Campion could have written it. And touching our Society, it said in its peroration, we have made a league, all the Jesuits of the world, whose succession and multitude must reach over all the practices of England, cheerfully to carry the cross you shall lay upon us, and never despair of your recovery while we have a man left to enjoy your Tyburn, to be racked with your torments or to be consumed with your prisons. The expense is reckoned, the enterprise is begun, it is of God, it cannot be withstood. So the faith was planted, so it must [54] be restored. Prejudice discounted, Campion's *Brag* remains one of the noblest, wisest and most indiscrete documents in English history. As far as Jesuits are concerned, the *Brag* remains domestically effective, raising very ordinary men over three centuries to a stature many inches higher than they would ever have attained themselves.

4

The mystery of
Robert Persons

[55] It fell to Persons, now in exile, to organize the Jesuit mission and implement Campion's *Brag*. He, after a year in the shadows of the gallows, left England never to return. Until the end of his life in 1610, he regretted that of the thirteen who set out on this work with him, all had either attained their reward, or were still undergoing their contest; he alone is left out for his sins. Persons was certainly right in his decision to leave England, though when he did he intended to return. The Jesuit press could not be continued there. Both Frs Williams and Hartley [56] were in jail. Persons had to consult with Allen about the proposed mission to Scotland, and there were others matters of business to be dealt with. Nor could he neglect those friends he had ordered out of England, especially Gilbert and Basset. After Campion's arrest the search for Persons redoubled, and his superiors refused to countenance his return.

The General, Claudius Acquaviva, had renewed misgivings about the whole mission that Mercurian had launched so reluctantly. The fears expressed at Southwark were now heard amongst Jesuits. It seemed wrong to send men to torture and death just to edify others and bring more reprisals down on the Catholic community. His enemies would accuse Persons of fleeing out of cowardice, [57] though in truth his intrepidity was not in doubt. Emotionally he suffered much. When Campion, Sherwin and Briant died at Tyburn in 1581 he lost three close friends and a fourth, George Gilbert, died of fever in Rome in 1583, having taken his vows on his death bed. Briant, a Somerset man like Persons, was probably closest to him. He had written a letter of exceptional beauty to him from prison asking to be admitted to the Society. On his capture he was questioned at length about Persons but he told nothing. He was twenty-eight when he was executed.   [58]

Persons was a truly enigmatic Jesuit, but two thirds of the charges against him may be discounted. Though for thirty years the British Government tried to blacken his reputation, history has unearthed no new accusations. The worst that could be said against him was said with no lack of venom three hundred and fifty years ago. In recent years many contemporary documents concerning his life have been discovered and two priest historians, Philip Hughes and Peter Guilday, not uncritical of Persons, have helped to correct the bias. The latter notes the literature on the subject is so impregnated with anti-Jesuitry, that its acid inevitably influences readers unconsciously.

Many of his plans were personal to him, not those of the Province or Society, so in this sketch they can find no place. Some Jesuits, Creighton and Tyrie, Manares, the   [59] Wallon Provincial and the Jesuit Cardinal Toletus, were critical of him. Yet popes and cardinals supported him; he rarely worked without the approval of his superiors, and as we have seen, a great number of reputable English priests admired and trusted him. The letters of John Bavant, the tutor of both Campion and Persons at Oxford, reveal that Persons cannot be seen as all black or all white. He who is often painted as the arch intriguer plotting to sell his country to Spain was the son of a yeoman from Nether Stowey in Somerset. At the Taunton free school for boys he surpassed his fellows. His enemies later challenged his parentage, but among others old Mrs Persons, at ninety, said a thing or two about that, as did his brother, an Anglican clergyman. Typically English, Persons seems   [60] far more blunt, conservative and predictable than Campion. Though widely travelled in Europe, he was always an exile, almost a jingoist. Oxford University, English clergy, Douai Seminary, the faith of the English, were the best. At no time did he desire Spanish dominance, though with Allen he believed that most Englishmen were at heart Catholic and would welcome outside help to free them from Tudor tyranny. West country and yeoman in outlook, Persons had less cunning [61] than simplicity. His strength and weakness was that he could not shift his position or alter his opinions in thirty years. He held to the deposing power of the Pope without compromise, while theologians were trimming their sails. He was too simple and single-minded for a complicated and double-crossing world. Besides Cecil, Walsingham, Essex, and the other trimmers, he now seems hopelessly direct. Many of his Catholic adversaries – William Gifford was one – saw no great problem in accepting emoluments from the Spanish and English side. The staff at the papal nunciature was not beyond a bribe. Persons in a true sense had no price. He was fully committed to his course, which was the traditional Catholic position – recusancy

Friend and enemy alike admit the astonishing influence [62] he had but few take the trouble to explain this fact. His enemies could not shift him. They attributed all to cunning and dishonest practice. Yet one of his virtues, as one of his most malignant of his modern critics has admitted, was his charity, his compassion for men of every type, for the frustrated seminarians in Spain and their superiors, for the students at the English College in Rome who averred that they at first saw him as their enemy, but admitted he proved their greatest friend. He was kind to those who betrayed him, or who were difficult or disordered, he was generous to the poor, assisted the exiles, the English prisoners, priests in trouble.

Persons made a massive contribution to the Catholic [63] cause. Whatever he did his actions stemmed from a mature plan. His *Christian Directory* was ranked a classic for three hundred years. His Protestant opponents produced a version free of Catholic error and corruption. By the time of his death it had gone through four editions by Catholics and fifteen by Protestants. He is credited with thirty books under various pseudonyms. According to Fr Richard Holtby, citing the Earl of Salisbury, his elegance and the simplicity of his style give him a foremost place among English writers. He was also an energetic printer and publisher, setting up the press that he had established in England at Rouen. Now he could keep up the pressure. He preferred, as Gilbert tells us, books of small compass, otherwise they would not be read or bear fruit. Some [64] books served a double or triple purpose. *De Persecutione Anglicana* not only recorded the heroism of the martyrs but helped fashion public opinion in Europe and raise funds. Other Somerset men would take over from Persons: John Gibbons and then Dr Bridgewater, one-time rector of Lincoln College Oxford. Persons, after inspiring the venture, moved on to other work. [65]

Young John Gerard, aged about seventeen, enters our story at Rouen when Fr Derbyshire brought him to meet Persons who was busy with his press. Gerard writes in his biography that he spoke to Persons about his vocation and wish to join the Society but he was still very weak and could not continue his studies. Persons suggested he return to England to recover his strength and settle his affairs. As Good had inspired Persons so Persons inspired Gerard. Persons, with the printing press established, could [66] give his mind to the English mission, which was in a parlous state. Campion and Briant had joined Pounde and Mettam in prison, Cottam was captured; allowed to escape he only enjoyed a short liberty and was duly hanged. Bosgrave was also arrested and, knowing nothing of religious conditions in England, agreed to attend the established Church. It was sometime before he recognized his mistake. He published a disclaimer, was jailed and appeared with Campion in the dock but he was not hanged. He lay in prison for three years and was exiled.

Despite Persons' protests, Jesuit affairs in England were
[67] allowed to drift for two years. The General would send no
new men and Jasper Heywood found himself the only
Jesuit priest not in jail. The mission had its problems.
Fr Thomas Langdale, a middle-aged man, returned,
announced himself papal envoy and attended Protestant
services. Fr Christopher Perkins had been dismissed from
the Society and returning to England, became Anglican
Dean of Carlisle, married the aunt of the Duke of Buckingham, was knighted by James I and went on diplomatic
missions for the English government. In the years 1581–83
Persons was on diplomatic missions which brought him
no joy, although he made a lifelong friend of Philip II of
[68] Spain. The hesitancy of the Jesuit superiors regarding the
English mission remained, as can be seen from Persons'
despatch on such missions. Only in the autumn of 1583
[69] did he return to the Channel coast. Now he could give his
whole mind to one task. First he had to find suitable rein-
forcements. Middle-aged men taken from other work and
sent in unprepared were unsuitable. He wanted Henry
Garnet, a young professor of mathematics in Rome, Robert
Southwell, a student of great intellectual ability and a
close friend of his, Richard Holtby and John Currie,
secular priests who had crossed from England to join the
Society. These four, with John Gerard when he was ready,
would provide a more solid foundation for the future of
the enterprise.

In the meantime he had to work with what he had.
Wiliam Weston was suitable but Thomas Marshall, who
pleaded to go, was not; Persons would have let him go
because of his earnest goodness, but the General would
not have it. A careful study of the alternative Channel
crossings was made so that his men might have a safer
passage. Eventually four routes were used. Emerson and
Weston would sail from Dieppe and come ashore between
Lowestoft and Yarmouth, Garnet and Southwell would
land east of Folkstone, Oldcorne and Gerard at Cromer.
Tesimond and Ashley would sail from Flushing to

Gravesend. Eventually priests, nuns and children would travel to and fro with impunity. Not long after Persons' death, a spy reported that a papist merchant, Mr Skult, had conveyed sixty priests via Rotterdam, St Valery and Hamburg. Disguise was needed. Blount and others came [70] from Spain dressed as returning prisoners of war; he himself appeared before the Lord High Admiral and so impressed him that he was awarded a financial indemnity.

Persons wrote to the General on 15th September 1584 telling him that Weston and Emerson had left ten days ago. He arranged a special boat for them and managed [71] also to have an English gentleman enter with them and guide them safely to his house. They were well primed and clothed, their expenses paid and they had seventy crowns in their purse. It is not easy to convey the full scope of Persons' work, finding suitable men, shipping them to England, and procuring money and supplies, all of which he did. Shortage of funds was perennial but in all financial matters he was generous. He begged and gave unceasingly. He lived simply, with English spies watching every movement, and survived one or two serious attempts on his life. His safety measures proved a success. Weston avoided arrest for two years, Southwell for six, Henry Garnet and Edward Oldcorne had eighteen years of freedom and Blount and Holtby were never caught in forty years. The only casualty now was Emerson impris- [72] oned for nineteen years, and emerging paralyzed down one side. In 1586 Persons saw Garnet and Southwell off from Rome to England. Garnet proved a shrewd adminis- [73] trator and acted as local superior, Persons retaining general control, though less directly concerned with the mission. In Rome in 1586 he made the Spiritual Exercises for thirty days and took his final vows. He was forty and had been a Jesuit for ten years. In Rome he saw that Allen was made Cardinal, to honour him and encourage the English exiles. Allen was delighted and admitted Persons' share in obtaining him the honour. In 1588, Persons set off for Spain.

As a result of his own academic career and of his lasting friendship with Dr Allen, Persons had seen the importance of seminary education and the significance of Allen's success. The foundation of seminaries for English students became his all-absorbing aim. In all he established four [74] and hoped to found another in Italy. In his dreams about a restored English Church, he visualized a great college in London to which students would throng from the continent, thus England, in the tradition of St Boniface, would give back the faith to northern Europe. In that restored Church seminaries would have the status of universities and theological degrees would be very hard to come by. All his plans were based on the assumption that the conversion of England would be achieved by the learning and holiness of its priests.

In Allen's and Persons' reckoning, the usurping government would soon be forced to come to terms. From what they knew of English Catholics they were certain that Elizabeth lacked popular support. They were less concerned about training seminarians in exile, more with providing [75] trained priests for when the day of deliverance dawned. As each hope faded another took its place; Mary Queen of Scots, then her son, then the question of Elizabeth's successor. The bravery of the Catholics, the number of crypto-Catholics, the success of the priests from Rheims and Douai, confirmed their highest hopes. In 1611 an Italian gave property in Madrid for an English college, to revert to the Spanish Jesuits when the English went home, and in 1637 the Petre family planned a Jesuit college in Oxford. Such hopes grew less substantial but were they no more than wishful thinking in Persons' day? He and his contemporaries saw France change her allegiance when Henry IV decided Paris was worth a Mass.

It was one thing to recognize the need for seminaries, and another to provide for them. In 1585 there were two hundred in the seminary in Rheims, many maintained only by borrowing, some were middle-aged, some school-[76] boys. Overcrowding, lack of discipline, inadequate funds was the result. As it was, many unsuitable candidates were admitted in Rheims and Rome and some became government informers or spies. A further cause of unrest was the employment of foreign Jesuits in English colleges, good men but ignorant of English idiosyncracies. Allen and Persons were not deterred; both were grateful to foreign Provincials who supplied for the lack of well-trained Englishmen. Within a few months of his escape from England, Persons had established his first school at Eu which could take twenty boys. It survived ten years until the seminary moved back to Douai and he opened his College at St Omers. Persons set off for Spain in 1588 on Jesuit business. From there he suggested ten students should be sent to Spain, and when he heard a group of students had arrived in Valladolid, he obtained a pension and hospice from the Spanish king and established an English College there in 1589.

A dual interpretation may now be given for all Persons' actions. The orthodox view is that of Allen. Persons, he [77] said, has always been my faithful helper in supporting the common good of our country and of God, who has used him as an instrument for the foundation of English seminaries in Spain. A far different verdict would be given by some of those involved at Valladolid, who describe the little community as living quietly there when Fr Persons appeared and trouble began. One fact is certain, the students came to Spain just after the defeat of the Armada when Englishmen were not popular, some of this group being arrested seven times. Persons gained for them security. The mystery of Robert Persons is emphasized. Of [78] those early students Henry Floyd, John Blackfan, Richard Blount, Andrew White, Thomas Garnet admired him greatly and became Jesuits. John Cecil, John Bennet, William Atkinson and Dr Richard Smith, a professor, would rank among among his most persistent enemies. Persons certainly slaved for the College. There were thirty students in 1590, seventy-five in 1592, the year another College was founded at Seville. The teething problems of

these Colleges were painful; climate and diet were particular problems. The health of many was impaired, and not
a few died. To raise funds Persons published two books,
got a licence to import and sell English cloth, and took
students with him on money-raising missions.

Persons kept in close touch with English affairs and the
[79] threat, never carried out, that Catholic children over the
age of seven would be taken from their parents and
educated as Protestants was enough to drive him to the
completion of a project which may have been in his mind
for many years – a college for English boys at St Omers in
Flanders. He decided to send Henry Walpole as a missionary to England and by this means obtain from King Philip
a farewell audience, which he did, and he received a royal
charter and a promise of funds. In his plan Persons
expected Douai to send recruits to Rome for the English
College, while St Omers would supply the Spanish seminaries. The first boys attended classes at St Omers in
October 1593: they were seven – four Worthingtons and
[80] three Rockwoods. Typically Persons probably himself
never visited the College; William Flack was left to tackle
the immediate problems and Henry Walpole assisted him.
Tragically Walpole sailed for England in far too great a
hurry and in the wrong ship. He could not be landed on
the Norfolk coast within easy reach of family protection as
intended; instead they put him ashore at Flamborough
Head. He was arrested on landing on 5th December 1593
and was hanged two years later at York, aged thirty-seven.

Boys who went to St Omers made no promise to be
priests. If any decided they would, they went from St
Omers to Valladolid. Boys were admitted at fourteen.
They had to be English or from Greater Britain; if living in
exile, both their parents had to be English and Catholic. A
knowledge of Latin was obligatory. The problems facing
[81] St Omers were great. The Spanish authorities resented the
payment of an annual pension, and Persons had to make
up the deficit. The magistrates of St Omers resented an
English college in their midst. English troops were aiding

the rebels in the Netherlands so this college seemed a security risk. The Walloon Jesuits were also indignant. They had a flourishing college and hardly welcomed an English school in the same street. To allay all such discontents the King ruled that the rector of the English College must be a Belgian. The troubles at St Omers faded with the appearance of Fr Giles Schondonch, a Walloon, as rector, for this warm-hearted and generous man, an Anglophile with a love for music and spending money, ironed out the troubles between the Walloon and English Jesuits and established those traditions which would survive at St Omers for a century.

Three unsolicited tributes were paid to St Omers, [82] Robert Persons' most enduring work. First, English agents sent reports on the College in 1594 and reckoned the students numbered fifty. Next, in 1608, two years before Persons' death, Bishop Blaise of St Omers, a Franciscan, visited the college, of which he proved to be a devoted patron and friend. The final tribute is more telling, penned as it was by a doughty and honourable adversary of the Jesuits, Dr Matthew Kellison, President of Douai, who sent a secret report to the papal nuncio in 1622. The object of the community, he informed him, was to keep the Colleges at Rome and Spain supplied with students every year, and this work has been splendidly done; sixteen or twenty or sometimes more were sent each year, youths most promising in Greek and Latin scholarship and excelling in virtue.

Cardinal Allen died in October 1594. To his personal [83] merits, learning, piety, and doggedness may be added his personal social advantages, his seniority, and high ecclesiastical preferment. Though his political theory varied nothing from the views maintained by Robert Persons, those who attacked Persons awarded Allen a strange immunity. One modern writer, by no means favourable to Persons, expresses it this way. The affection and reverence of such priests for Allen personally led them to judge him in this matter too gently and to lay the blame too indiscriminately upon his Jesuit friends and advisors. For nearly twenty years Allen had been Persons' protector and his personal friend and in a true sense, Allen had created Persons as a public figure. Their mutual respect and sympathy were genuine. Over a score of years misunderstandings between them were rare. Yet after Allen's death stories were put about that the Cardinal had grown weary of the intriguing Jesuit. One Catholic pamphleteer hinted [84] that Allen's death was not quite normal and that the Jesuits for good measure had also poisoned Owen Lewis, Bishop of Cassano, and Pope Sixtus V.

With Allen's death, Persons found himself increasingly isolated and more bitterly attacked. For three years following the loss of his friend he remained in the Spanish Colleges while two parties among the Catholics intrigued to get their candidate into Allen's place. Persons never sought the honour, and indeed rejected it. These squalid rows had their amusing side. When Persons asked his brother George to procure some red flannel for a bodily ailment, the merchants of Rome delivered bales of scarlet silk to the English College. Persons returned to Rome in 1597, for some students were in revolt. He settled the grievances with tact and skill and remained in Rome for the rest of his life. He still watched over the English mission, St Omers, and the seminaries in Spain. Mounting hostility to his policies embittered his declining years but without distracting him from his main purpose, the education of future priests. His capacity for work and close attention to small details made him a formidable adversary. He was always a move ahead and we have from a government agent a description of Persons at his desk. He has notice in twelve or fourteen days of all that happens in England. He receives his letters on Wednesday and on Thursday calls his secretaries, Walpole, Smith, Stephens and John Wilson [85] who write continually till midnight on Saturday.

Was he as wicked as his enemies suggest? The appellant controversy seems never ending. Only a handful of Jesuits and some thirty seminary priests were directly involved in these skirmishes. Persons' adversaries were not drawn from any social group. At the head stand two personal rivals: Dr Christopher Bagshawe, like Persons a convert, had been an enemy of his at Oxford, and Dr Owen Lewis, later Bishop of Cassano, who was involved in the original disputes at the English College between the English and the Welsh. Both had their circles of friends. Next come a group of seminary priests numbering about thirty in 1598. Some of them had been mischief makers in their seminary [86] days. It would be unfair to condemn them for this but Persons had some excuse for suspicions about them; he would dismiss them as the malcontents. This was his mistake because some were honourable priests who had worked and suffered in England for many years. Colleton had stood in the dock with Campion, Mush had applied to join the Society, Thomas Wright had been a Jesuit for years.

Aiding and abetting these priests were members of the French party, including the French ambassador in Rome. The wholehearted Spanish policy of Allen and Persons drove their opponents into the French camp. Behind all these were the English statesmen, with money available, only too anxious to fan the flames. To offset the appellant clergy Persons could claim many senior English priests: Bavant, Campion's tutor at Oxford, and Blackwell, one of his collaborators on his early books. Fitzherbert, first a widower then a priest and finally a Jesuit, was devoted to Persons, as were Drs Barrett and Worthington, Presidents of Douai after Allen. Of Jesuits hanged for the faith in this period, Briant, Cottam, Thomas Garnet, Morse, Filcock, Corby, Arrowsmith, Cornelius and Page had come to the Society as secular priests, while Blount, Holtby and Andrew White were drawn to the Society in Persons' day. Would mature men, living in danger, have entered the society had Persons been evil as some of his adversaries tried to suggest? Finally Persons had behind him the Jesuit General Acquaviva, a great many cardinals and the popes [87] themselves.

The attack on his Spanish policy was less vicious and personal than the charges brought against him for his treatment of the seminary priests. He was accused of blocking the appointment of bishops in England because these might curb the power of the Jesuits. He was said to have taken control of two seminaries and to be trying to govern Douai through his friends. He used the seminaries as a recruiting ground for Jesuits. The seminary priests had borne the brunt of the persecution and had produced more martyrs than had all the religious orders put together, and yet after the coming of the Jesuits, whom they had so fully welcomed, these seminary priests found themselves despised and dispossessed. The Jesuits by toadying up to the rich, and vaunting their special privileges, had gained money for their Order and safe shelter for themselves. Seminary priests, deprived of their chance of a university degree through the policy of Persons, were now ignored by the laity. The Jesuits by their plots and intrigue, by their intolerance in doctrine, by the very fact of their arrival in England, had provoked the government and brought bitter persecution to innocent, peace-loving [88]   secular priests.

Though many of these charges were false and others grossly exaggerated, no Jesuit reading them today can escape a sense of sorrow and regret. One may wonder why Persons, a man of so much sympathy, failed to give any credit to the honest intentions of these adversaries. The answer lies in this, the appellant priests were not just airing local grievances. Running through all their literature is a common attack against the Jesuits' great design. It was the contention of Dr Bagshawe and others that almost since 1579 when they achieved power at the English College, Jesuits were scheming to dominate the secular clergy and grab all the influence and money for themselves. Grievances could easily be found to support this. Persons' enemies went back beyond Balliol, to his childhood in Nether Stowey to find evidence of latent cunning and intrigue. His friendship with Drs Barrett and Worthington at Douai became part of a scheme to dominate secular priests. Allen's promotion of the cardinalate was just another trick. The students were living peacefully at Valladolid when up popped the ubiquitous Jesuit. One excerpt from the *Memorial Against the Jesuits* [1597] must suffice to express the basic hypothesis of Appellant literature. It said the Jesuits that are in England are desirous either to bring under bondage, or utterly bear down the clergy of the Church of England. First their will is that in every Catholic house they may be pastors. And if there be any that will not obediently execute the things they have commanded they shall be censured as apostates or tainted at least by some heresy.

Persons, his many friends, the cardinals, failed to heed the genuine grievances of some of the appellant clergy for [89] they too were working to a hypothesis. Persons saw behind the acts of his adversaries another great design. He was well aware that some of his opponents – Bagshawe, Watson, Cecil, Bluet to name but four, were in touch with the English government. To Catholics who had suffered repression for so many years, whose recusancy had cost them the full severity of penal legislation, such behaviour on the part of priests looked very like apostasy. At a critical time when the united Catholic party might wrest concessions from the old Queen or her successors, it would pay the Establishment in England to split the Catholic vote. Persons may have been wrong, but at least he was consistent; on his hypothesis the clerical malcontents were either mischief makers or dupes.

Through the nine troubled years from the death of Allen to the accession of James VI of Scotland two contradictory explanations of Persons' motives may be adduced. No adjudication is attempted here. If as the appellants thought, Persons was working for the aggrandisement of the Jesuit Order, then every detail of his strange behaviour could be readily explained. So one exaggerated phrase culled from one of thirty books, that the Jesuits were the salt of the earth, would be dutifully copied by enemies over the centuries. His equally moving praise of the seminary priests never had the same publicity. Any rebuff in Rome by any appellant was due to Persons' jealousy. That the said appellant had been released by government connivance and been give government protection to collect funds for the Roman delegation, was no excuse for [90] Persons' angry attitude.

Here then was the battle of hypotheses. The controversy burst into flame over the appointment of bishops for England and to every appellant it was clear that Persons was preventing any such appointment lest bishops should curb the pretensions of Jesuits. Only in more recent years has it been remembered that the Jesuit General Mercurian expressly asked for bishops in 1579. The old Bishop Goldwell failed to make the journey, and later chided the Pope for the delay in providing bishops. Persons certainly favoured them at the start and in 1597 proposed two, with twelve archdeacons to administer the various Provinces. To his enemies this was a typical Persons trick. The arch-[91] priest Blackwell was nominated and immediately blame was heaped on Persons. Blackwell was his crony, had authority only over the secular clergy and was ordered by Rome to consult with the superior of the Jesuits. Blackwell was certainly a friend of Persons and the twelve assistants were priests of the same conservative type.

The appointment in the long run proved unsuccessful. The appellants wanted a bishop friendly to themselves. Persons himself points out that an archpriest might give less offence than a bishop to the English government. George Blackwell was not an unworthy candidate. One of the leading appellants, Dr Ely, said that if it had been a [92] question of electing a bishop he would have given voice for him as soon as for anyone else. The fact that he was a friend of Persons led to his unpopularity. Yet looking at the list of possible candidates, one looks in vain for anyone who would have been acceptable to both sides.

The sincerity of the majority of the protagonists need not be questioned, for most based their behaviour on hypothesis. For the appellants the start of the Jesuits' great design to lord it over the secular clergy began in the Castle of Wisbech, where a group of prisoners were living happy and godly lives when William Weston started his sly efforts to become superior. The same design of the Jesuits to get control after the death of Allen was seen in Rome in the English College and in all Persons' efforts to calumniate the secular priests. This hypothesis would damage Robert Persons' reputation for centuries. Whatever his power in his lifetime he certainly lost the battle after his death. Cardinal Manning was of the opinion that the Jesuits from Robert Persons downwards have hindered the restoration of the Church in England, a mysterious permission of God for the chastisement of England. Manning, however, though disapproving, was always courteous to English Jesuits. [93]

The case for Robert Persons has never been given in full. In the first place non-Catholic historians for three centuries wanted to know nothing good about him; and the appellant hypothesis supported the Protestant cause. Father General Mutius Vitelleschi imposed a ban on controversy and whenever it was lifted the Jesuit protagonists, though learned, lacked both publicity and skill. The first sign of an open defence of Persons is found in *The Tablet* where in 1844 an anonymous writer attacked the [94] third volume of Dr Tierney's *Church History*. In more recent times Peter Guilday and Philip Hughes, Catholic historians of distinction, while criticizing Persons, clear him of many crazy accusations levelled against him in his day. Such a defence remains negative. It is hardly sufficient to show he was not as wicked as his adversaries contend. His contribution to the Catholic cause, second only to Allen's, raises him far above the level of many of those who sniped at him. Whether or not he was intolerant, pigheaded, interfering, by sheer determination, in adverse conditions, he created a remarkable system for the future education of priests. Those who dislike the Church or Counter-Reformation must dislike him but there is no need to be unfair to him.

Since the turn of the twentieth century much accurate contemporary material has been published. Most important of them is a full collection of the documents relating to the Wisbech stirs. Dr Bagshawe no longer has the field to himself Now we may read both sides of the famous controversy, the views of Weston, Pounde and others together with Henry Garnet's admirable defence of himself. Here too are printed the examinations of Fr Robert Fisher, a forlorn but important witness of the cause of the troubles in the English College in Rome.

The complexity of the dispute is thus brought home, the deliberate activities of mischief makers, the part played by the English government in fostering the disputes. The evidence in support of Persons' grand design to humiliate and master the secular clergy is met by other evidence to illustrate the type of organized opposition against which Persons had to contend. The editor of the *Wisbech Stirs*, writing of Fr Robert Fisher's contacts with England, sums up thus. His coming provides proof of the link between Bagshawe's party in England and two small circles among the English Catholic exiles, one led by the layman Charles Paget and by Dr William Gifford, Dean of Lille in Flanders, and the other by Hugh Griffin, Provost of Cambrai, Nicholas Fitzherbert and others in Rome. The characteristic of these three groups was animosity against the English Jesuits and one of their main aims, according to their avowed intentions, was to secure the Jesuits' exclusion from the English mission and from the government of various seminaries. The means were varied; fomenting disturbances in the English College in Rome, campaigns of calumny against the English Jesuits, spreading propaganda for schemes of liberty of conscience which were to depend on the Jesuits expulsion from England, and fostering dissensions between Jesuits and other religious. Similar plans formed the constant feature of the proceedings of the appellants.

Two deductions can be drawn from the evidence,

[95]

neither of which concerns Robert Persons. The English government had all to gain by sowing discord inside the Catholic body and the Pope needed no advice from a Jesuit to recognize the danger of allowing the appellants to [96] select a bishop for themselves. As for Persons, the mystery surrounding him is not yet dissipated, but while any Jesuit who wishes is free to do so, no Jesuit need feel obliged to hang his head.

5

Digging in

The effectiveness of the Elizabethan persecutions varied [97] considerably from place to place. The lord of the manor was at that time still his own master and influenced those who lived on his estate. Justices of the Peace and mayors had wide discretion and London required their full co-operation to produce an adequate effort. In London a stranger drew little attention, in rural England a visitor soon became a talking point. Priests, to avoid detection, had to match their plumage to the soil.

Campion's tactics had been tragically unsafe. The government had been warned of his arrival and the priest hunters missed him by minutes many times in his adventurous year. Once he was saved when a maid pushed him into a pond. News of his journeys went before him. He had only to return for a second night to a previous lodging and he was caught. Eliot the priesthunter, posing as a papist was gladly admitted by the unsuspecting cook at Lyford Grange and he was taken. With Campion in jail and Persons fled, only Jasper Heywood was at liberty, [98] newly arrived and hiding in Staffordshire. Persons sent him a message appointing him temporary superior of the mission.

Fr Jasper was not the failure his enemies made out. We find him assisting two men who would perish in the Tower of London; Philip Howard, Earl of Surrey and

Edward Percy, Earl of Northumberland. He proved elusive. Fr Richard Holtby, riding South, could not find him and crossed to France to consult Fr Derbyshire. On 16th April Heywood writes to Dr Allen that he had been endeavouring to find a special messenger to send to Rome. Hitherto that had been not possible. He greatly rejoiced that other soldiers were being sent to reinforce him. [99]

Fr Jasper fell foul of his fellow Catholics on the subject of Friday abstinence. English Catholics resented the recent mitigation of the fasting laws. Not so Fr Jasper who, at a meal in which pious Catholic friends were devoutly abstaining, put away a dish of meat. The outcry was immediate and shrill. The Jesuit General found it neces- [100] sary to order Fr Jasper to come to Rouen to explain himself. He dodged the priest hunters and sailed for Dieppe but an unfavourable wind drove the boat back to England and he was imprisoned in the Clink. He was brought to trial, but the Lieutenant of the Tower came to Westminster Hall and removed him before it took place. Rumours followed the extraordinary event. The guess nearest the truth is that influential friends intervened. [101] Fr Jasper had been reared at Court, his father had held a most honourable position there as a playwright and had belonged to the family circle of Sir Thomas More. Jasper lay in the Tower for a year; William Weston records his suffering. In January 1585 he was banished from England to spend the last fourteen years of his life in Italy and France.

William Weston crossed to England in September 1584. [102] His companion Ralph Emerson was caught at the customs but Persons had anticipated all possible disasters and Weston had the address of the Bellamy family at Uxenden near Harrow. On his arrival in England he showed consid- erable courage, visiting Jasper Heywood in the Tower of London, who informed him that all the prisoners knew about his crossing and that the Queen's Council had been informed. Weston went straight to ground. His caution showed in his dealings with the Earl of Surrey, Philip

Howard, whose interest in Catholicism had been fired by Edmund Campion.

The Earl arranged a suitable secret meeting for the reconciliation so that the household did not know about it, and a day or two later at a private place, in the presence of a few relatives, Mass was said and Communion received. At the request of his Superiors, Weston wrote a full length [103] autobiography. Simple, naive, half stage Jesuit, half vicar, his was the innocence of Fr Brown. He had his scares, a spy at Mass, a prolonged search for priests, Weston on a ladder, with his head through a manhole, listening for hostile footsteps, saying his brievary. In his quiet unassuming way he took he first steps to organizing the English Jesuit mission, compiling a list of country houses in which Jesuits might hide. As he one day became the hero or the villain of the Wisbech stirs, his autobiography is of some importance.

One trait alone in Weston's character make one suspi-[104] cious of his stability: his excessive interest in demonology. Such a preoccupation, salutary within bounds, must surely have coloured his judgements and may explain the violent reactions against him. One fact is abundantly clear: Weston enjoyed a high reputation for sanctity. His autobiography leads one to believe he was a very devout and dedicated Christian with a pious attitude to life and nothing is more irritating to those who are less pious than the presence of an officially holy man.

Some days after he had got back from this journey he was told that two Fathers had arrived in London. The persecution at this time was very severe and in the midst of all these anxieties it was a great consolation to him, he tells us, to have faithful and brave companions, so he went to the inn where they were staying. They were Henry Garnet and Robert Southwell. There being no safety in London they went thirty miles to visit Hurleyford near [105] Marlow from 14th to 22nd July. This interlude is unique in that the missionaries need not have worried about their safety. Their host, Robert Bold, had in his house not only a chapel but both choir and orchestra. William Byrd was one of the party, of which the climax would be a *Missa Solemnis*. For Catholics of this period such an interlude proved an abiding joy.

A number of distinguished laymen came to Hurleyford on this occasion and among them was one of the most devoted of the Jesuits patrons, Lord Vaux. For the first time in many years an effort would be made to distribute the incoming priests. Since 1581, 150 had been sent to England of whom about thirty had been executed and another thirty lay in prison while others drifted about London in a forlorn and unprotected state. At the same time Catholics in the provinces were deprived of the sacraments. Ten years later, despite the most savage [106] counter measures, a network of private houses across the country offered shelter for three hundred priests. The credit for such a scheme, founded on the generosity of laymen, seems principally to belong to Lord Vaux. It was the Vaux family who, immediately after Hurleyford, took Southwell to their house at Hackney and gave Garnet shelter at Shoby in Leicestershire. At the Hurleyford house party the three Jesuits took council. Weston showed Garnet and Southwell his list of suitable houses; they in turn had new instructions from Rome. Garnet is named superior, should Weston be captured. Five days after Hurleyford he was. He gives us the full story of his arrest, his year in the Clink, the move to Wisbech where he found Ralph Emerson, Thomas Mettam and Thomas Pounde. Mettam was a sick man and he died in 1594. [107]

Whatever our verdict on Wisbech few will approve the outcome of these bickerings. Dr Bagshawe, deliberately it would seem, involved his opponents with the government. If Fr Giles Archer is to be believed, Bagshawe's hatred of Weston went as far as this. Weston was imprisoned in the Tower for five years, in solitary confinement, suffering greatly from insomnia, headaches, blindness and loneliness. His constancy and patience were impressive. He was released and expelled from England and in 1603 and arrived at St Omers in a terrible state. Yet he recovered speedily, returning to Spain in easy stages and nine years later was made Rector of the English College in Valladolid, being sixty-five when he died in that post in [108]   1615.

With the arrest of Weston, the English Jesuit mission was near to collapse. Garnet became superior, though he had been in England for barely a month and knew nothing of penal day conditions. Nor was he cast in the role of a pimpernel. Son of a Nottinghamshire schoolmaster he had been trained in Hebrew and mathematics, subjects with no direct bearing on the tasks ahead. As far as numbers were concerned, the mission was declining. In early 1581, Campion, Persons, Emerson, Holt and Heywood had all been active. Now in 1586, only the raw recruits Garnet and Southwell were free. True there were men in Rome training but sending English Jesuits to other countries had not stopped; William Wright was in Austria for example. Few could have foreseen in 1586, the remarkable expansion which would raise the number of English Jesuits to three hundred in forty years.

The Jesuits had no monopoly of virtue, neither were they masters of deceit. Friends who exaggerated their courage paid them a disservice, while their enemies by calumnies and falsehoods made giants of ordinary men. Of the 182 men and women executed as Catholics under Elizabeth, eleven at most could be classed as Jesuits. Of these only Campion, Walpole and Southwell were Jesuit trained. The other eight were seminary priests who had [109]   asked to be admitted into the Society. On Fr William Holt's reckoning in 1596, six hundred priests had been sent to England in thirty-eight years. The Jesuits, after sixteen years in England, could claim at the most twenty-five. With such figures before him Fr Philip Hughes could poke fun at three popular assumptions. First the Protestant fear of Jesuits lurking behind the wainscott of every popish manor with their omnicompetence in crime. Next he needles the Catholic partisans who saw the Jesuit hand in every triumph, and a certain type of Catholic critic who see it in every catastrophe.

Such wise observations preserve our sense of proportion; they hardly answer the point. How are we to explain the rapid Jesuit expansion at the turn of the seventeenth century? Hughes and Guilday stress the advantages of the centralized Jesuit system while the seminary priests, [110] without bishops lacked both coherence and a rallying point. The appellant priests would explain the Jesuit expansion by their hold on the seminaries. Such charges can now be checked. In the first twenty-four years of the college at Valladolid – to cite one example – out of 199 students, thirty-three later joined the Society; of these thirteen became Jesuits only after working as seminary priests.

Several facts help to explain the sudden expansion without discredit to anyone. The first is the influence of the Spiritual Exercises. A second contributory cause may be found in the dilemma facing recusants in the wake of the Armada of 1588. It presented to the English government a ready-made excuse for further severity and the Catholics with an impossible situation when they came before the courts. The decisions confronting them were [110] more agonizing than those met by collaborators or resistance leaders in the war against Hitler. Catholic collaborators gambled with eternity. Religious issues rend the conscience and lead to double dealing. Many people conformed in public but supported a Catholic priest in private in case of sudden death.

Three groups may be distinguished in the Catholic body, [111] disintegrating under pressure from these events. A large number apostatised. Next there was the valiant minority, who were ready to face death, imprisonment and ruin rather than disown that which they thought to be true. Between the two, many by faith adhered to the old religion but with mounting misgivings as to the wisdom of the policies of sixteenth-century Rome. On the deposing power of the Pope, on the morality of taking the oath of allegiance and of attending heretical churches, Catholics were divided. After 1588 the English government could more easily work to widen the gap between the two factions. Rumours of plots abound, distinctions drawn between the peaceloving and the trouble makers, with the Jesuits, still [112] only a handful, the bogeymen. Garnet expressed the situation in a letter to Acquaviva in 1590: The fact is that we are guilty of no treason other than upholding Catholic doctrine. We are questioned, tortured, flayed, we are put to death unless we declare that we are willing to take up arms against the Pope in any circumstances whatever.

Not all Jesuits were orthodox. The attitude of Fr Thomas Langdale and Christopher Perkins in an earlier decade would be found again later. Fr Thomas Wright, after leaving the Society, entered into negotiations with the Earl of Essex under promise of security. It was broken and he was thrown into jail, but tried to rejoin the Society. This was not to be, so he remained long in England and hostile to his former colleagues. His extraordinary career illustrates the confusion of thought among earnest Catholics. In 1606 his brother Fr William Wright was brought from Austria to England to serve as the learned champion of Roman orthodoxy.

In the main the Jesuits kept close together and accepted outright the current Roman attitude. Once in the *Annual Letters* mention is made of a dispute among the Fathers about the Oath of Allegiance, but nothing came of this. Their education made Jesuits Roman as a matter of course. Professed Fathers in the Order bound themselves by a special vow to such obedience, but all Jesuits were taught to think with the Church. This expression, so dear to their founder, meant thinking with the Pope. Sin excepted, the Jesuit was pleased to leave himself at the disposal of his Superiors and these were pleased to carry out the wishes of the Vicar of Christ in Rome. A type of pride, peculiar to the Marines, is found in Jesuit letters: as one Protestant pamphleteer put it, the Jesuits were the horns of the Papal [113] Bull.

Though they were to suffer greatly for this, such unquestioning loyalty brought the Jesuits a great number of devoted friends, who were ready to risk life and wealth for the support of priests and Catholic doctrine; Pounde, Gilbert and his friends, Vaux, Petre, Brinkley, Fitzherbert, Bellamy and many others. Philip Howard, Earl of Surrey was first drawn to the Church by the sight of Campion in the Tower. The charge would be made against the Jesuits that they busied themselves with the wealthy people. The Jesuits certainly worked for every class but their ability to do so derived from their friendship with the rich. Whether with rich or poor the Jesuits made no friends by diluting doctrine but by their very conservatism. Their own uncompromising recusancy bought them uncompromising friends. These it was who kept the Jesuit mission alive, provided alms and shelter in England, support for the College of St Omers, their sons to swell the ranks of the Society. [114]

Given devoted and uncompromising friends, the Spiritual Exercises of St Ignatius began to produce in England, despite the persecution, the same results as were seen on the Continent. A third condition was also present and deserves attention, for in the closing years of the century they were directed by outstanding men. Philip Hughes ranks Southwell and Campion as the finest flower of their generation and groups Garnet and Gerard with Persons as personalities who must have stood out above their fellows in whatever age they lived. Southwell was an outstanding poet. Even after six years in hiding and a traitor's death at Tyburn, he achieved an honourable position in the golden age of poetry. In appearance he was boyish and extremely handsome. With such good looks went an ardent character and a passionate desire for friendship. Seasoned men like Derbyshire, Garnet and Gerard express towards him an exceptional love. Even the battle-scarred Persons sends messages to my well beloved Robert Southwell. When Southwell came to England he was loved by Vaux, the Bellamy and Arundel households; when it came to

[115] imprisonment and torture he aroused in Topcliffe a vicious form of sadism. After he had been hanged, the London crowd paid tribute to this inborn attraction – the beauty of his face and form so won the hearts of all that even the mob gave it their verdict that this was the properest man they had ever seen that came to Tyburn. Garnet [116] reports all this.

From adolescence Southwell had cherished the desire to die a martyr. The surprise with him lies in his practical resourcefulness. Until he came to England he was diffident. Yet his friends were later to be astonished at his *sang froid* during the years he lived in London and in his appalling sufferings in jail. Except for one long excursion into the English countryside, he seems to have lived for six years inside London's square but sacred mile, Moorfields, [117] Holborn, Fleet Street, Bridewell and the Strand. He had an admirable hiding place in Arundel House and an unusual friendship with the Countess and Philip, Earl of Arundel, a prisoner in the Tower with whom he corresponded. Southwell knew he was bound to be caught and he was betrayed by Anne Bellamy, daughter of one of the staunchest of the Jesuits friends. In prison for her Catholicism, she left it pregnant, some say by Topcliffe himself. She may have warned Topcliffe who came in person to arrest him. That was in 1592; he was hanged three years later. In the three years he was moved from jail to jail, was briefly in the Tower, was always in solitary confinement, and was cruelly treated by Topcliffe, who had permission [118] to torture him at his house.

In the Tower he was the near neighbour of Philip Howard, the Earl of Arundel but they had no personal contact. A Jesuit, probably Garnet, was present at South- [119] well's execution in 1595. The death of Southwell was an overwhelming blow to him for Garnet was a shy man who did not easily make friends. In his letters to General Acquaviva he expresses the intolerable burden of loneliness that he had to carry for nineteen years. He was always a wanted man during the most savage years of persecution. Yet he built up an administrative system with breathtaking insouciance. Garnet was in a sense the first resident Superior in England for Heywood and Weston had been Superior in name only. It fell to Garnet to establish those traditions of religious observance that would survive for centuries.

Southwell opened the first hostel for priests in London. [120] Later Garnet leased many houses in the London suburbs to protect his men. Persons had set all his hopes for the Jesuit mission on Garnett – and his judgement proved correct. Tributes to his prudence, charity, and shyness are paid by Southwell and Gerard whose safety was in his hands. Oswald Tesimond, recently arrived from Spain, had been with Garnet two or three days when he was warned that the Privy Council knew of the house in Moorfields which would be raided that night. Fr Henry, without being the least bit afraid, bid them recommend the necessities of the house to Our Lord and, after taking [121] some refreshment to strengthen them for the ordeal, told them to get ready as best they could. They then went one in one direction, another in another. Some showed signs of fear and reasoned that it was impossible to escape. Fr Henry remained calm, gave orders to hide, in the places long prepared, everything that showed that the house belonged to Catholics. Lastly when it was dark he sent away those that were guests or strangers, that they might return to their usual dwelling places. His object was that they should go together to another house he had in London which he kept for such emergencies.

Garnet's programme was to welcome new priests to London and the first two he welcomed two years after his own arrival were John Gerard and Edward Oldcorne, the second of whom he escorted across England to Worcestershire. Two veterans landed in the north in 1590, Holtby and Currie, both having completed their noviceship. Holtby remained in the north while Currie went to Chideock in Dorset, later to Cowdray in Sussex; he died in John Gerard's house in London and was buried there. A painful part of a superior's work turned on the frequent executions sometimes of Jesuits, often old friends. When he could not go he had to arrange another priest to do so and send him an eyewitness account. The sight of the executions and the tension of his life told heavily on Garnet especially – those of Roger Filcock, a Jesuit, Mark Barkworth, a Benedictine, and Mrs Anne Line, John Gerard's patron in 1601. Yet he survived four more years, [122] greatly admired by all who worked for him. His principal task was both spiritual and domestic. Now at last the spiritual rules worked out by Mercurian were put into practice. It is not generally understood that the first Jesuits who came to England had not yet completed their training. Persons pronounced his last vows in Rome in 1586. Garnet was professed while acting as Superior in England; Oldcorne and Gerard when they landed on the coast of Norfolk, had only been Jesuit novices for a few weeks. Blount was a novice when he made his sensational escape from Scotney Castle. Page had applied to join the Order and was at Gerard's house in London when he was caught. He took his vows as a Jesuit on the morning of his [123] execution in 1601.

The moral dangers for all priests in England were very great. Fear, bribery, idleness, lack of supervision and discipline, were a constant threat. Many former priests became government informers, some attempted marriage, some entered the Anglican ministry. The Jesuits had their failures but thanks to Garnet's elaborate safeguards, the general standard remained remarkably high. In their first hectic year in England Campion and Persons met regularly for confession and renewal of their Jesuit vows. Southwell and Garnet met at stated times for the same exercises. It was Garnet who extended and organized this practice as the Jesuit numbers increased. In 1591 disaster almost overtook the English Jesuit mission at Baddesley Clinton when priest hunters arrived while all the those in England were in the chapel to renew their vows. Southwell was about to vest for Mass: vestments and the rest had to be stowed away while Anne Vaux in her night attire engaged the searchers till all the priests had disappeared. Gerard wrote that the hiding place was below ground level and the floor was covered with water. Fr Garnett was in it as also were Frs Southwell, Oldcorne, and Stanney, together with two secular priests and two or three laymen.

After this the Jesuits could not meet so often because numbers were increasing and Garnet could not risk all his men in one place. Smaller groups were formed, eventually eleven of them, with two weeks a year assigned to each. The programme was silence for three days, then a conference by one of the priests, High Mass, part of the breviary recited in choir, an exhortation by the superior of the mission and on the final day, renewal of vows. Garnet's [124] achievements were never as spectacular as Gerard's, but not only did he succeed in building up small, embryo communities in various districts, but he inspired these with loyalty and discipline. When Gerard put the matter of his intended escape from the Tower to Garnet, he replied that he certainly ought to attempt it but should not risk his neck in the process. Not all Jesuits were as easy to handle as Gerard, Weston and Southwell. Thomas Lister, [125] an outstanding scholar in Rome, proved a prima donna on the English mission, a mischief maker and hypochondriac. Garnet's kindness to Lister shows us the type of man he was. He remained patient with him and twice sent him to Flanders for a rest. Eventually he returned to and worked happily in England for twenty-five years, mainly in the Oxford district, of which he became Superior. The strain of [126] the mission which eventually would undermine even Garnet, played havoc with Thomas Stanney, a simple and pious priest who came to England in 1586 and there joined the Society. In fear of betraying his patrons he moved to an inn. There, in a delirium, thinking that Protestants and Catholics were enjoined in battle, he knifed a chamberlain. The examining magistrates declared him deranged. He was imprisoned for twenty years, his fellow Catholics

esteeming him a Saint. Banished, we may smile to hear he
was appointed Prefect of Health at St Omers, an office he
[127] held for eleven years.

The expansion of the English Jesuit mission was therefore due to three remarkable men: Garnet, Southwell and
Gerard. It is more difficult to apportion credit between
them. Garnet and Southwell, without John Gerard, would
have shown few concrete achievements, while Gerard on
his own would still have proved a success. His was the
[128] drive, theirs the prudence; they trained him, shaped him
to the Jesuit pattern and gained by his initative. Garnet
was a professor of mathematics, Southwell a poet, Gerard
showed himself a resistance leader to the manner born.

The Jesuits never produced his like again. Indeed they
cannot claim to have made John Gerard. He was still only
a novice in 1588. His autobiography shows him alert,
impudent and resourceful from the day that he first
crossed to Europe at the early age of thirteen. He had met
Persons in Rouen, returned to England and appeared in
the courts. He tasted a spell in prison and witnessed the
cruelties practised on prisoners in the Bridewell, long
before he applied for the priesthood at the English College
in Rome. Gerard in his audacity and singleness of purpose
resembles Lawrence of Arabia. He thrived on danger,
reacted spontaneously to every challenge and hardship,
inspiring others by the virility of his self confidence. Small
wonder that his sparkling biography has proved a best-
seller for he tells his story without pride or self pity,
fearlessly and factually.

In every house or prison in which he stayed he immediately took the lead. Other priests were hesitant on landing.
Gerard, chasing his fictitious falcon took about ten
minutes to make his first friends. On his first days in
England he acquired a horse and fixed himself up with
friends in Norwich, after which he rode to London with
two horses and a servant of his own. Garnet was not
amused. Gerard describes the warmth of his welcome. but
Garnet later issued an order reminding priests who

arrived in England that they should call on the superior at once. Assigned to one house, Grimston, Gerard was invited to another and then a third. In every residence he won the affection not only of the household and of the servants but of the neighbours, Catholics or non-Catholics. After a few years in England he could count on a welcome in any part of the country and tells us that on all his travels he never had to lodge at an inn. In jail he converted two of [129] his jailers, a great many prisoners, and so many came to see him that he reckoned he did more good in prison than when free. He hunts, plays cards, uses duplicate keys, invisible ink, wears frills and feathers and is once tempted to draw his sword to chase the priest hunters down the stairs. In prison he delights in outwitting magistrates and jailors, and enjoys polishing and rattling his chains. Not only was he brave under torture but later could analyze his thoughts. With his fingers still numb, he could risk crossing the moat of the Tower of London clinging to a rope.

With this panache Gerard remained, beneath the surface, a cool and determined man. He had only one purpose in life: the defence and extension of the Roman Church. He never forgot he was a priest. In an age in which so many lived double lives and suffered scruples, Gerard's simple faith and confidence in God made him a formidable director of souls. As he moved from house to house he left behind him in each new centre a priest to take his place, Jesuits, or one of his friends among the seminary priests. The houses he opened in London were shelters and hostels for all priests. He refused alms and gifts from the majority of his clients, yet accepted large sums from a few dedicated friends.

His greatest achievement was his marked ability to speak without shyness of spiritual matters. He was the ideal retreat director. Other Jesuits were shy of women. Gerard drew his penitents from both sexes and every class. He admits that he had less success with heretics than [130] with the schismatics, those crypto-Catholics who feared to declare their faith. We note that John and Thomas Wiseman, Michael, Edward and Christopher Walpole, Robert Lee, Thomas Smith, Willam Sutton, Thomas Strange, Nicholas Hart, Henry and Francis Page, from Gerard's circle, not only recovered their faith but went on to be priests. The case of Page is extraordinary for this handsome convert was brought to see the Jesuit in prison by his Catholic girl. So great was his attraction that he came day after day to Tower Hill when Gerard was in the Tower to doff his hat and bow facing Gerard's cell.

Gerard built up a network of devoted servants all of whom suffered greatly as his confidants. Anne Line, a widow, took charge of his London House for three years. Richard Fulwood, a Warwickshire businessman, was captured in mistake for Gerard and lodged in the Bridewell. Despite his sufferings he escaped when Gerard was in prison and acted as Garnet's man of business for [131]   years. When in the Clink (1594–7) Gerard had Ralph Emerson in the next cell, and John Lillie, an apothecary in the cell above, turned it into a chapel. Gerard bribed the jailer and said Mass there. In the Clink, Lillie and other prisoners made the Exercises with Gerard and this changed his life. He served as his confidential agent, smuggling letters, bribing warders, bringing visitors to the Tower to see the priest. He once, by clever acting, was taken to jail in his place. Both Lillie and Fulwood eventually entered the Society as brothers. Nicholas Owen was [132]   another of Gerard's close friends. He was an Oxfordshire man, a carpenter who had helped Campion and Persons and made hiding holes so effective that he saved hundreds of lives. During the day he seems to have worked as an ordinary joiner, building hiding holes by night in every part of the country. He was imprisoned after Campion's arrest in 1594 for being a papist, and was admitted to the Society as a lay brother some years before his death. When Gerard planned his remarkable escape from the [133]   Tower of London in October 1597 Lillie, Fulwood and Owen brought the operation to a success. Lillie and

Fulwood steered the boat to the Tower jetty and Lillie climbed the wall of the moat to draw the crippled priest to safety. Fulwood stood at the appointed place with two horses to effect the escape of Gerard's jailer. Owen was ready with the other horses so that Gerard might also ride away. In the boat with Lillie and Fulwood was the former jailer from the Clink. [134]

In November 1605 the Gunpowder Plot was officially uncovered but so well had Garnet laid the foundations of the mission that his own removal was not an irreparable loss. Richard Holtby was made Superior and the number of recruits did not lessen, nor did Jesuit influence in the Catholic body decline. The Jesuits never took the plot seriously. The heretics had striven to render the very name Jesuit hateful to fix upon them the odious name of sham plottings. Garnet and Oldcorne were captured at Hindlip on 27th January 1606. Garnet left a vivid description of the six days in the hiding place. Both priests had resolved to perish there rather than betray their friends. They might have escaped detection had not Owen and Ashley been forced to emerge from another recess. Oldcorne and Ashley were hanged at Worcester. Oldcorne was a simple, ponderous Yorkshireman whose bluntness amused Gerard. Ashley had been a baker in Valladolid; he returned to England because of sickness and became a Jesuit.

Owen died on the Tower rack without speaking. It was [135] announced that he had taken his own life. In fact he had had a rupture: anxious to get his secrets, an iron plate was tied to his stomach and he was tortured till he died. Garnet was said to have to have confessed to a knowledge of the plot, told him by Tesimond under the seal of confession, to have shown no bravery when faced with torture, and that in confession to Oldcorne, tapped by government agents, he had accused himself of being drunk. Caraman offers some evidence that Garnet had been drugged while in the Tower. Much was made of his use of equivocation. Garnet's reputation was blackened over nineteen years, not only by the

English government but by a small group of appellant priests. His defence of his government was written in 1597. Garnet died bravely; his demeanour on the scaffold strangely contradicted all stories told about his behaviour in his cell. The Jesuit party has always admired him. For some other Catholics, doubt remained about his prudence. His secret knowledge of the plot, though shrouded by [136] confession, suggested to some he was a conspirator. Before he died he wrote to the king apologizing for not revealing what he had known about the plot outside of confession, and in a letter to Anne Vaux he acknowledged that he died not a victorious martyr but a penitent thief.

In 1897 a Victorian Jesuit, also a John Gerard, but a Scotsman not a Lancastrian, challenged the traditional yarn. He was a man of unusual erudition and Professor S. R. Gardiner, a leading Stuart historian and David Jardine, a distinguised lawyer and editor of a series of State trials, answered him. Gerard questioned the access to gunpowder, the digging in non-existent cellars and the happy accident that killed off all the leading conspirators before they could testify. Both admitted the skill of Gerard's charges and were forced to make certain admissions, but in those days no gentleman challenged the integrity of an [137] English government. The attack was allowed to lapse.

Hugh Ross Williamson returned to it with his *Gunpowder Plot* in 1951 which resumes the arguments to a world less interested in English history and its honour, and more familiar with confessions under torture, Reichstag fires and government sponsored conspiracies. The facts were once more placed on record and one can honestly doubt the truth of the Gunpowder story. How far was the whole story contrived by the government? Garnet, Owen, Oldcorne, and Ashley were executed. Stanney, Weston, Emerson sent into exile. Tesimond escaped, as did Lillie and Fulwood, while John Gerard went to Flanders for a period of recuperation on the day Garnet died. All the old guard had now left England, by hanging, exile or flight, save only Richard [138] Holtby and, still in prison, Thomas Pounde.

6

Underground

The Jesuits after the Gunpowder Plot were not unduly unsettled but were faced with a long siege after the execution of Garnet. The modest hopes of the Spanish match of 1623 came to nothing and the battles with the Puritans of James I and Charles I meant that the recusants could expect no favours. The Jesuits were now featureless men. Should we conclude they were less talented and able than in Campion's day? It is a hard question to answer. Political conditions had changed and, with [140] rapidly rising numbers they had an elaborate system of seminaries, missions and colleges to maintain There was only one Jesuit, Holtby, free in England in 1608, but two years later there were forty. By 1633 there were, in what was now in an English Province, 364 men – a figure that would stay constant for a century.

Persons had established a regular system of command and gradually built up the strength of the mission. After 1598 its Superior stayed in Rome, with deputies governing communities in England, Flanders and Spain. There were three modes of living for those in England. Some lived entirely in one place, others were constantly moving about while others could be either at home or visiting others. The first group lived in the upper stories of a house or its attics. The same room contained altar, table and bed, and they had to be careful not to betray their presence to domestics or visitors. If they left the house they did so in the second or third hour of the night and returned when the domestic staff had retired. It could happen that, in a family of sixty or eighty people, they spent entire days or weeks alone [141]   except at Mass and a short space of time after or before it. A female servant brought dinner and supper then left. The lady of the house, or her children, might look in. They rarely saw any other Jesuit or priest. Those who travelled between places did so on foot or horseback, usually staying in one house for some days, being available to reconcile and minster to the people, then moving on. They were exposed to special dangers but saw fellow Jesuits more often and were encouraged by their being able to minister to the people.

More fortunate were those based in one place where their host was so esteemed by his neighbours that he could escape the action of the law, and where the servants were [142]   mainly Catholic. Superiors normally lived in such houses so they could move about to visit their subjects, or summon them to come to them, but by 1646 the Civil War had broken up families, and many were reduced to the first mode of living. Fr Thomas More, Provincial at the time, once found fourteen of his brethren, mostly [143]   displaced, cramped together in a small hut. There were moments and excitements at times of crisis, but loneliness, and boredom were the main problem for them as Fr Edward Knott, Provincial in 1655, noted. They sought to live near their relations, feeling that unless they were travelling, catechizing and preaching they were wasting their time, forgetting that the chief work of a priest is to say [144]   Mass.

Many priests had much trouble as newcomers, in getting established. Fr Thomas Laithwaite arrived in 1604, was captured and condemned to death. His brother gained his release and he was put on a ship for France but a storm placed him back in Hampshire, where he applied to enter the Society and was accepted at about the time of the Gunpowder Plot. Caught again he was banished. After doing his noviceship in Flanders he was back again, caught and jailed again. When being shepherded to the coast and exile again he got away, returned to London and was betrayed once more and jailed. He escaped again and this time stayed free, working in London 1621–49 and died there in 1655 at the good old age of seventy-seven. By [145] contrast, Michael Alford was caught on arrival in 1629. He was soon released, worked in Worcestershire for the rest of his life and visited libraries across England while researching *Annales Ecclesiastici et Civiles Britannorum, Saxonum, et Angloruma*, a very learned tome.

In each region of England after 1600, one Jesuit seems to [147] have established himself as the unofficial founder of the mission centre, and in some cases the official Jesuit Superior. In the north east where the persecution had been so severe, the veteran Richard Holtby administered the Jesuit mission for fifty years. Holtby had known Alexander Briant at Oxford as a young seminary priest, acted as host to Edmund Campion, and crossed the Channel in 1583 to make the Spiritual Exercises with Fr Derbyshire. He completed his noviceship at Verdun and passed to Pont a Mousson for further studies. He returned to his native Yorkshire in 1589. One of the toughest Jesuits who came to England, he never had a day's illness and he was never arrested in fifty years. He was an expert gardener, mason, carpenter and turner. He constructed hiding places and also made vestments. He was also highly spiritual, and directed Mary Ward, a Yorkshire girl. He had many close shaves with the pursuivants at Thornaby only escaping by lying motionless in the undergrowth for two days and nights. Thanks to his flair for friendship, the English Jesuits in the north east had enjoyed greater liberty and companionship. Mrs Dorothy Lawson, a wealthy woman, persuaded him to give her and her maid a retreat. She first [148] thought of becoming a recluse but was dissuaded from that. Instead she built a very well protected sturdy house, with an elaborate chapel, on the banks of the Tyne. At Christmas there were three Masses, and Holy Week

ceremonies were done with great splendour while half a
dozen Jesuits came to do their retreat there each year with
collegiate form and discipline, she providing all things
necessary. She also attended all the Masses each day. She
invited her guests to stay for a day's recreation when the
retreat was over, and was delighted to dine with them: the
night before they departed she gave a feast to the whole
household.

At the turn of the sixteenth century the majority of
Jesuits had been seminary priests. Holtby was one, and in
Lancashire there was another, Edmund Arrowsmith. He
lived as a Jesuit for four years, much loved by the local
Catholics. Betrayed and hanged at Lancaster in 1628, over
[149] three hundred years later he was still venerated. John
Bennett, educated at Douai and a contemporary of
[150] Holtby's, was founder of the mission in North Wales. He
had grown up in the neighbourhood of Holywell, fled
overseas as a boy and was one of the first of Allen's priests
to return to Britain. He was arrested in 1582, exiled in
1585, entered the noviceship at Verdun in 1590, and
returned to be welcomed by his old friend Holtby at
Newcastle, en route to resume his work in North Wales.
When he was seventy-five years old, he volunteered to
nurse the sick in the plague in London and there died on
Christmas Day 1625.

Robert Jones was another Welshman. He arrived at the
English College in Rome in 1582 from the Diocese of St
Asaph and entered the Society a few months later when
[151] aged eighteen. As a student and then lecturer in logic he
displayed that peculiar brand of intolerance so marked a
feature of the English College in his day. Disputes about
the Jesuits covering two decades made many of the
students on either side politically conscious, and also
partisan. Holtby and Bennett of an earlier generation were
free of this.Yet Jones was a highly efficient and in many
ways delightful man. The High Sheriff of Herefordshire
had a different opinion. To him he was Jones the Jesuit,
the firebrand. His principal supporter was Frances, the

fourth daughter of Edward Somerset, Earl of Worcester, whom he had reconciled to the Faith. Since the family had lands that had once been Church property, she agreed to support two Jesuits in the north, and two in South Wales. Jones was both courageous and prejudiced. With considerable bravery he visited Roger Cadwallador, a condemned seminary priest in Leominster jail, but he noted that none of the seculars had visited him and adds that the priest bequeathed his only possession, his library, to the Society. Jones, on the Jesuit side, represents the contentious spirit of protagonists such as Dr Richard Smith. The enthusiastic streak made Robert overwhelmingly Jesuit; it also made him intrepid as a missionary. The account of his death in 1615 tells of his injuring himself on an errand of mercy, and going on to another one before his wounds had healed. This resulted in more injuries from which he did not recover.   [152]
                                                                      [153]

In 1626 there were 152 Jesuits in England, at least half of them in the southern counties and east Anglia. In Winchester Thomas Pounde resided in the house where he was born and in which he died. He had been released from prison after Elizabeth's death and returned home to educate his nephews. Aware of his promise to go into exile and live as a Jesuit, he was told by Jesuit superiors he was too old to make the journey. When he died, the Annual Letters gave his age as seventy-five years, out of which he had spent thirty in prison. It is thought that Persons received him into the Society, and that he had been responsible for the Jesuits coming to England. Campion averred that Pounde's publication of his *Brag* did wonders on their behalf. The Queen, at whose Court he had, when she was young, been the idol, knew well how he desired martyrdom and was not going to render him glorious.   [154]
                                                                      [155]

The greatest of the Jacobean Jesuits is Richard Blount, who was never assigned a district, left no address and during forty-seven years in England was never caught, although an attempt was once made to take him outside the Spanish embassy, but in error Fr Blackfan was

[156]   arrested. Blount was born in 1565 of the Leicester branch
of a distinguished Anglo-Norman family. He became a
Catholic while at Oxford, went to Douai and was ordained
in Rome in 1589, the year in which students were sent to
Spain; there he met Persons who would after play a dominant part in his life. He tended to do everything well; he
was calm and courteous, he had a will of iron, was conservative and orthodox and had small sympathy for the
appellants. He crossed to England with ten others in 1591
and we find him living with the Darrel family at Scotney
Castle in Kent from which, probably in 1597, he made a
celebrated escape. He had been disturbed in his sleep and,
clad only in his breeches barely made it to the hiding
[157]   place. The pursuivants then searched the house for ten
days, while he and his man lived on a little bread and a
bottle of wine.

Taking the opportunity of a stormy night and darkness
they escaped, got over two walls ten feet high, on to a
broken tower about sixteen feet above the moat, and leapt
into the water. They made their way to a cottage,
borrowed clothes from a husbandman and walked fourteen miles to the house of a Catholic gentleman where Fr
Blount lay for three weeks, his feet and legs inflamed.
Typical of him, he left no account of his adventure; one of
the Darrels did so and it was discovered, some one
hundred and fifty years later, among old papers in a
drawer.

At the time of his escape he was a Jesuit novice, taking
[158]   his vows in 1598. One confidential report on him says he
was 44 years old, had finished his theology among the
first, had good health and remarkable experience, had
laboured well, was in great esteem amongst the principal
Catholics, very able, fit for government and for all the
[159]   duties of the Society. He was made superior of the mission
in 1617 and held various offices over twenty years. In the
wider world he had a strange immunity, on one occasion
being received by King James I at Salisbury, was an intimate of Queen Anne of Denmark who in her day had been

Lutheran, Calvinist, Catholic and Anglican. He was also much loved by Charles I's Queen Henrietta Maria. Blount converted the Lord High Chancellor, Thomas Sackville. There was also a story of his friendship with George Abbot, Archbishop of Canterbury.

Blount's most striking achievement was in a sense domestic – the establishment of a Jesuit Province in England in the face of opposition from Protestant and Catholic. Until 1593 the English Jesuits had owned no property. When Persons in that year opened the College at St Omers, for the first time it could be said that they did. [159] Then in 1604 Persons, using the 12,000 ducats bequeathed by Louise de Carjaval, acquired a fine property in Louvain. In 1607 the first English noviciate was opened. The first to arrive was Fr Thomas Garnet, nephew of Fr Henry. John Gerard bought the next property in Liège, the chief benefactor here being William Browne brother to Lord Montacute, helped by Sir William Stanley and Sir George Talbot, John Gerard's relatives. William Browne entered the order as a brother and died at the college he had founded in 1637, a victim of charity while nursing those stricken with plague. [160]

This college at Liège, acquired as a noviciate, later became a house for higher studies and the novices moved to Watten outside St Omers. The donor of the house at [161] Ghent (for the Jesuits third year of probation) bought in 1621 was Anne, Countess of Arundel, Robert Southwell's benefactress and friend. Thus in twenty-eight years the English Jesuits in Flanders had opened houses at Louvain, Liège, Watten and Ghent. Until Fr Blount and others estab-lished an English Province, however, these houses were not directly linked with the Jesuits in the English mission field. Other English Jesuits lived in Rome at the English College and others were busy with the two English semi-naries in Spain. A third abortive seminary was planned for Madrid in 1610 when Caesar Bogacio presented property to Fr Joseph Creswell but the houses in question were occupied by unfriendly tenants and Bogacio had died with many debts. Still Creswell came to Madrid with students and a papal brief; the new College was officially opened in 1611 but he made small allowance for mounting opposition, much of it fostered by the English ambassador. In the [162] end superiors ordered him out of Madrid in two hours.

Such problems would trouble English Jesuits in many places. Somehow they must obtain Provincial status. A Province enjoyed privileges and obligations similar to those of a diocese and the Provincial appointed by Rome exercised full jurisdiction over all his subjects and employed impressive faculties. A Province accepted novices, supported them and trained them, employing all its members in the way judged best. Finally a Province was entitled to send a delegate to Rome for the regular Congregations in which the business of the Society was [163] discussed. It fell to Richard Blount to show that somehow English Jesuits, hiding at home or scattered across Europe, could claim sufficient stability and permanence to form a Province. Two years after being mission superior he was in 1619 made Vice Provincial and began a series of administrative reforms. Henry More describes the problem thus. It is impossible for religious men to dwell safely together for an assembly of even an hour's duration without the greatest risk, so discipline suffers, they have no opportunity of meeting one another, and they are too far removed from superiors.

The first care of the Vice Provincial was to divide the island into districts and entrust government to superiors appointed for the purpose. This effort to achieve a regular pattern of religious life in the strange, unfriendly situation of Stuart England says much for the basic training of these early Jesuits. By 1620 there were nineteen of them in the district of London, eight in Suffolk, eight in Hampshire, in Staffordshire ten, in Lancashire twelve – the same number as there were in the district of Leicester. In Lincoln there were six, in York six, in Northamptonshire eleven, in Worcester five and in Wales eleven. In all there were 109 [164] Jesuits in England and a similar number in Flanders. Three problems faced the Vice Provincial if any Jesuit Province was to be recognized. The Spanish Regents of the low countries might object. Next, in England itself the regions with no colleges or houses must become self supporting. Five such fictional colleges were established, thanks to the generosity of friends who gave endowments, in London, Lancashire, Suffolk, Leicestershire and Wales. Eight residencies with fewer Catholics, smaller endowments, and not so many priests were added to these.

The greatest problem was the calling of a special meeting of forty senior fathers to elect a representative to go Rome to a gathering of Jesuit Procurators held every three years; the next was due in 1622. The mission, not yet [165] being a Province, had no right to be represented but the General, Mutius Vitelleschi, had invited it to send someone to explain its point of view. Like his predecessor, Claudius Acquaviva, he loved England and wanted to help Richard Blount and his persecuted men. Given the risks, the hostile background, the alertness of the Puritan party, the Consult, otherwise boring, acquires a brave, resistance atmosphere, with forty Jesuits united under the noses of so many spies and pursuivants. They availed themselves of the indulgence of the ambassadors of the most Christian King and assembled in London, because by international law palaces of ambassadors form a sanctuary. To it the Jesuits came in twos and threes led by trusty messengers, and they left the same way.

First they elected Fr Hilary Silesden to serve as delegate. Next they drew up a memorial for him to present. It [166] reminded the General of the secrecy in which they had to work. It mentions the older Jesuits who had laboured to the glory of God for twenty, thirty and forty years. Rumours have been spread that the English Jesuits will soon be withdrawn. With a man as resolute as Vitelleschi this was a telling point. The Jesuits paid public tribute to their friends in this secret assembly, saying that nowhere have benefactors shown greater love to the Society, especially since they could give nothing without running the risk of confiscation of all their goods and even of losing their lives. They have received the Society into their homes and provided all things necessary, founded houses for them first in a foreign land and then in England with a boldness beyond belief. Henry Silsden returned home with a pronouncement raising the English mission to a [167] Province, dated February 8th 1623.

Blount became Provincial and the General in appointing him returned to a favourite topic, that some competent person be appointed as soon as possible to collect in writing the glorious deeds of the sons of the Society. In England, Blount's administrative blueprint would survive 200 years. His so called Colleges were little more than names on paper with endowments to support a few Fathers. In London there was the College of St Ignatius, in Liverpool it was St Francis Xavier, in the district of Stafford or Lancaster one dedicated to Blessed Aloysius. It was not wholly by accident that in the nineteenth century the Jesuit school in London was called after Ignatius, that parishes in Worcester and Hereford should be dedicated to St George and St Francis Xavier, and that St Michael, Patron of the old Yorkshire district, should be honoured in the new grammar school in Leeds. The Province developed smoothly with the Provincial living secretly in England, while the Vice Provincial Henry Silsden governed the houses overseas.

The secrecy so vigilantly maintained was however shattered when in 1627 a building near Blackfriars, in which two or three hundred people had gathered to hear a sermon by Fr Robert Drury, a Jesuit, collapsed. Drury and many of his hearers fell to their deaths: another Jesuit [168] William Whittingham died with him. This tragedy revealed the scale of the pastoral work that was going on secretly. By contrast, in 1628 the discovery of the noviceship in Clerkenwell seems an accident due to carelessness. The Jesuits had planned a special festival for St Joseph's day and to avoid suspicion, food for the community had not been purchased locally. More, in his account of the incident, remarks on the jealousy of local tradesmen. As one of those arrested, he would have known of such local pettiness. On the other hand Sir John Cooke's account shows that the house had been under suspicion for some time. Cooke thought at one time that he had unearthed a [170] new Gunpowder plot or at least a potential threat to Parliament. The priests were taken off to different prisons and the books and furniture were taken away. Nothing remotely treasonable was discovered and after a brief period the Clerkenwell discovery was allowed to fade away. The experiment of an English novitiate was not tried again. [171]

Among the papers captured at Clerkenwell was possibly a letter from Blount. It touches on two of the problems troubling the English Jesuits. The fourth paragraph admonishes all not to meddle with anything belonging to the temporals of Mary Ward, or of her company, and make the world know that the Society has no more to do with them. Blount, following the General's instructions brings to an end a discreditable story. Mary Ward alone emerges with credit and she had to wait till 1909 for the first signs of grudging acceptance. A Yorkshire girl, born in 1585 of devout Catholic parents, Mary's first contact with Jesuits was through Richard Holtby, her confessor. Holtby did not at first approve of her desire to become a nun. He changed his mind after he had a spiritual experience while he was celebrating Mass and gave her a letter to the Jesuits at St Omers advising her to see Fr William Flack. Mary [172] crossed to St Omers in 1606 but she was interviewed by the wrong priest. Fr George Keynes saw her and wished her into the wrong convent. ·Later Mary returned to England to gather round her a lively group of equally attractive and talented friends.

With these she returned to St Omers, not to enter a convent but to open a school. Her success was bewildering and in a very few years she had schools in Belgium, England, Germany and France. In England her followers visited the prisons, nursed the plague stricken, educated Catholic children and assisted the missionary priests.

Mary had many friends among the Jesuits; her brother joined the Order and Edmund Neville, her youthful suitor, would die in prison as a Jesuit. Without doubt her greatest support in her early years was John Gerard. Identified with her in St Omers was Fr Roger Lee, a young Jesuit, who, as a layman had played a central part in John Gerard's campaigns. Now as a minister at the English college in St Omers, Fr Lee served as chaplain to Mary Ward and the English ladies.

[173] Opposition to Mary Ward was based on a variety of charges. In an age when all nuns were enclosed, Mary had in mind a new type of religious order, without habit or enclosure, its members, without the traditional safeguards, living under vow. Criticisms of such innovations are understandable even when not justified, yet misgivings remain and these Guilday was brave enough to make explicit. Her Institute was sacrificed, her good name lost, her reputation blackened. She was jailed by the Inquisition, her sisters cast penniless into the streets of Liège and all this because of the animosity of some of the secular clergy for the Society. This does not exculpate the Jesuits. True Mary Ward was ruined when her sisters were named Jesuitesses but the exclusive spirit of the Jesuits gave to such a nickname its point and viciousness. Jesuits, since the foundation of their Order, had always fought clear of a female branch. Men like Gerard, White and Lee might encourage the English ladies but Blount and Vitelleschi [174] were determined not to become entangled. John Gerard defended Mary Ward and was delated by a fellow Jesuit. In January 1628 he was commanded under holy obedience [175] to break all contacts with the English ladies.

Reference has been made to deep divisions inside the Catholic party. The basic issue was a grave one, for the power of the papacy in relation to bishops is still under [176] discussion today. A contemporary pamphleteer saw the fight as one between the Jesuits cherished by the court of Rome, darlings of the Pope who blindly do what he commands; the others, sustained by the Canons of the

Councils and obeying only according to the law. If the [177]
Jesuits were touchy about their dignity, a complementary
weakness was found in their opponents, described by
Monsignor Ronald Knox as a morbid exaggeration of that
jealousy on behalf of the secular clergy which you sometimes find among exemplary Catholics.

As Blount remarked, the Jesuits were on the best of
terms with many bishops in other parts of the world.
Three of the most illustrious of English bishops, Allen,
Challoner and Milner must be counted among the Jesuits'
most respected friends. The friction derived from the
legacy of bitterness from Persons' days. The turbulent men
on either side were making mischief, identifying the good
of the Church with partisan victory. Blount's letter is not
dated, but reference to the appointment of a bishop refers
to Rome's decision to send a vicar apostolic to England.   [178]

William Bishop was one of Persons' chief adversaries.
He came to England, dying within a year, but during his
short reign he set up a chapter and appointed vicars
general and deans. The priests of the new chapter
suggested names for his successor, Dr Matthew Kellison
President of Douai at the head. Perhaps he was passed
over by Rome because he was too anti-Jesuit, though in
fact his hostility was balanced and his great virtues might
have saved the day. In place of Dr Kellison, indeed over
his head, Dr Richard Smith was chosen and came to
England in April 1625. Of this new vicar apostolic Allison
remarks that though a man of many gifts, he lacked
precisely the qualities that were most needed, he was
doctrinaire, tactless and overbearing. One wonders that
Rome, with so many candidates to choose from, could
have made such a choice. The promotion was almost
certainly due to the intervention of Cardinal Richelieu,
with whom he had worked for a time in France. Almost
from the start of his pontificate in 1625, Dr Smith set about
the task of degrading the Jesuits. On the evidence of an ex- [179]
Jesuit expelled for grave moral offences, he accused
Gerard of having admitted his share in the Gunpowder

Plot. Allison hints that the General may have threatened to go to law over the calumny. In the end the charge was [180] dropped but with no amends.

A second case affected Fr Thomas Poulton. That Poulton had insulted Cardinal Richelieu was known in [181] Rome. His offensive remarks are trivial, written in a private letter to a friend in 1624. As some gesture had to be made to pacify Smith and the Cardinal, Poulton was dismissed from the Society. When Smith retired from England in 1631 the General gave permission for his re-admission and he died a Jesuit in 1637. A great many other silly charges were made against Jesuits and were sent to Rome. When Smith left England the English Jesuits must [182] have heaved a sigh of relief. The popes had often pleaded for an end to these English feuds and Vitelleschi decided to insist on silence, even in self defence. Only on one occasion in the eighteenth century was an exception made.

The troubles with Smith and the pressure to have Jesuits withdrawn from England may have helped Blount to take his last dramatic step. The question of a Catholic expedition to America had been raised on previous occasions. [182] Persons considered and rejected it in 1605. In 1632 George Calvert, Lord Baltimore, obtained a Royal Commission for one. English Jesuits had been debating the project since 1629 and Blount found the prospect of the mission in Maryland highly attractive, not only for its spiritual opportunities, but as an escape from the ceaseless Catholic hostility at home. Though nothing had been decided, Andrew White wrote to the General in 1629 to offer himself as a volunteer.

White had been a babe in arms in London when Campion arrived. At fourteen he was studying in Douai, went on to Valladolid and studied also in Seville, returning to England a seminary priest. Banished after the Gunpowder Plot, White entered the Society, and he was a [183] novice in Louvain with Thomas Garnet and Henry More. He professed scripture and theology for many years at Liège and returned to the English mission working in

Suffolk and Devonshire. Vitelleschi answered favourably [184]
and White acted as Secretary to Lord Baltimore. He was
made Superior and his companion was Fr John Altham.
Brother Gervase went with the original party and several
other Jesuits crossed the Atlantic to give temporary assistance. White was fifty-four when they sailed from Cowes
on 22nd November and he kept an elaborate log of the
journey which he later wrote up into a brilliant narrative,
rich in detail. Yet for White himself, a pious man, the final
paragraph is all important. On the Day of the Annuncia-
tion of the most Holy Virgin Mary in the year 1634 he
wrote 'we celebrated on this island the first Mass which
had ever been offered up in this part of the world.'

Foley, in his excerpts from the Maryland *Annual Letters*,
well depicts the hardships and courage of those early
years. Many of the early volunteers died young. Altham
perished in November 1640 of fever, Br Gervase was
carried off by an epidemic and with him Fr John Knowles,
aged thirty. He who had yearned for a missionary vocation, lived for just two months in Maryland. John Cooper, [185]
Roger Rigby and Bernard Hartwell, whose arrival in 1642
was greeted with joy in the *Annual letters*, all perished at
the hands of Puritan marauders from Virginia. They were
all in their thirties.

Philip Fisher, the Jesuit Procurator in London, acted as
agent and attended to supplies. In 1637 he sailed to
become Superior of the mission, leaving White to work
more directly with the Indians. White achieved great
fluency in their language and published a grammar,
dictionary and catechism. After marauders from Virginia
destroyed the mission, he was brought back to England
with Fisher. Put on trial for their lives the Jesuits were
acquitted on their plea they had not returned to England
willingly. Fisher returned to Maryland. White was
released in 1648 and shipped to Holland without papers,
crossed to Flanders and turned up at the Jesuit house in
Antwerp. The old man wanted to return to his Indians but [186]
superiors would not allow it. Instead he was sent to

England as a chaplain to a family and died peacefully in 1656 aged seventy-seven.

As Provincial Blount was directly involved with many delicate problems. The General raised a favourite topic that a competent person be appointed to collect in writing the praiseworthy deeds of the sons of the Society. Blount was scrupulous in this, in the preparation of the *Annual Letters* and the annual inspection of accounts. His visitation of the houses in Flanders was first carried out in 1622. He had to report the heavy debts borne by Fr Schondonch, the admirable rector whose passion for music and drama had brought the house a high reputation at the cost of studies. Blount decreed that a school play should never last more than two and a half hours. In letters to and from Vitelleschi we follow the story both of, for example Mary Ward, and John Gerard's journey across Europe; we also see the General asking what a Scottish Jesuit, Fr William Christie, was doing in London and ordering Blount to [187] send him on his way. The unhappy college at Madrid was causing trouble and Frs Forcer and Price were quarrelling. The noviciate at Watten was restless because Fr Creswell was too old to change his methods of government. Creswell was made superior of the house of third probation because no Fathers would be coming that year.

While Creswell was too aggressive, the young Father Edward Knott was too shy. The general wanted this talented man for promotion but he rejected the thought. Knott eventually held many posts on the continent: Superior of Watten to undo Fr Creswells errors, next Superior of all Belgian Houses, in 1624 Master of Novices, and then Master of Tertians after John Gerard. He acted as Blount's deputy in Flanders with great success, but, asked to be [188] rector of Liège in 1628, he completely lost his nerve, went to Rome and was arrested on his way home. Two years in the Clink completely restored his confidence. Blount, and Knott his understudy, managed a smooth running of Jesuit affairs. In letters to the General and from the General one gains the impression that the government of the Jesuits was extraordinarily efficient and that human nature has not changed much over the centuries. Blount was sick in 1626, and needed a rest. In 1633 he asked to be relieved of office and in August 1635 the General agreed. Blount died in 1638 and Henry More succeeded him. Here was the passing of an age. Holtby [189] died in 1640 as did Fr Thomas Fitzherbert; the last two English Jesuits who had known Campion. Henry More belonged to another world. He first appears as a handsome little boy in the college of St Omers at the time the Countess de Zueda visited the place. Seeing him, a pleasing boy of the family of Sir Thomas More, she embraced him with maternal affection, adopted him for her son in order to provide maintenance and education, and next morning gave him a brass crucifix.

7

The road to Tyburn

Henry More lived at Chelmsford in Essex, as chaplain to the Petre family at Ingatestone Hall. He was probably twice in prison; he was certainly one of the party caught at [190] Clerkenwell. John Gerard, under whom More served as assistant novice master, judged he would eventually be qualified for governing. He was not a great success on the staff at Liège as his temperament was better adjusted to England in persecution times. He is the first official historian of the English Province. His great tome *Historiae Missionis Anglicanae Societatis Jesu* compiled in hiding holes, [191] was finally published in 1660, the year before his death.

During More's Provincialate most London Jesuits lived in the suburbs. A limited number lived inside the walls of the city, with well-established patrons or foreign embassies. Conditions for Catholics in London had changed greatly since the days when Persons saw priests being dragged as prisoners through the streets. Executions were rare as Charles I groped hesitantly towards religious toleration and his Queen, an attractive and pious Catholic, did all in her power to assist hunted priests. Henry Morse, when threatened with arrest, could openly seek her aid. Archbishop Laud was kindly and well intentioned. One odious feature of English life that remained was the power given to informers and pursuivants; for information leading to arrest they could earn as much as £50. Several lapsed priests found the trade lucrative and knowledge gained in seminary days now stood them in good stead. They knew the recusant families and could recognize and identify their former friends. Catholics were often [192] provoked to anger by such treachery. Henry More describes how his friends drew their swords on an informer and would have pursued him to his death had they not been entreated to turn from that purpose.

The Jesuits could not retaliate, though they occasionally express relief in their *Annual Letters*, as when one pursuivant was felled with a pewter pot in a tavern brawl. [193] 'Catholics,' they tell us, 'are reduced to the greatest misery, there being no security for persons in place or time from the fury of these harpies.' Yet the work of the London Jesuits expanded smoothly. Pastoral work had to be done in secret; the tragic collapse of a floor in Blackfriars building, in which some died, disclosed a large mixed crowd of some 200–300 gathered listening to a sermon; most were very ordinary folk.

The *Annual Letters* supply the General with endless statistics about spiritual triumphs, the number of general confessions, and conversions, but they touch also on the sadder side of things, the attending on the death of a convicted criminal who received absolution at the end. A charming feature of the *Letters* is that all undertakings succeed. Pastorally the plague-stricken became an urgent [194] matter. In 1625, London suffered a severe attack and dangerous epidemics were a regular hazard. At first all Jesuits laboured for the plague-stricken but as the risk of contagion grew two priests, a Jesuit Henry Morse, and a seminary priest John Southworth, were set apart for this harrowing mission. Relations between these two heroic men were strained at the beginning on account of the wrangles between seculars and regulars but thereafter they worked well together in the grim conditions. They boldly and publicly appealed for alms and Queen Henrietta gave much support, yet informers were ever active and both eventually were executed.

A small group of Jesuits worked in central London. The Province Procurator had his offices there. One, John Ireland, was hanged at Tyburn on charges brought by Titus Oates. The Maryland mission's agent and that of the Scottish Jesuits was also in central London as was Br Cuthbert Prescott, from the College at St Omers, who escorted returning schoolboys and attended to books and fees. He never coped with less than two hundred boys a year, mustered his flock from every county and guided them to and from St Omers despite government spies. He seems to have been in prison many times; and he was in Newgate when Fr Corby was taken out to execution. He himself
[196]   died in there in 1547 aged fifty-five.

One enigmatic priest, Edward Astlow, deserves a mention in this section. Roger Filcock had reconciled him to the Church at the age of fifteen and he studied at St Omers through his kindness. He went to the English College at Rome and became a Jesuit in 1608, serving as private secretary to Blount and then More. In the letters of Vitelleschi, Astlow is mentioned with great praise. On several occasions he seems to have begged to be relieved of his office but when More became Provincial he particularly asked for his services and the General agreed
[197]   conditionally. In 1644 we find him making one last dangerous Channel crossing and he died two years later on the Continent.

Another group of Jesuits were busy with the work of the St Omers press. To take the St Omers side first, the press itself was in working order when the Bishop of St Omers visited the College in 1608. In charge was Fr John Wilson. A secular priest, he lavished his money on the English College and the boys. A later Provincial would say he was so great a benefactor to the Seminary at St Omers as to have merited the title of founder The press was a very modern one by the standards of the day as was recognized by Fr Vitelleschi, when deciding to print the first authoritative version of the Jesuit Institute – three thousand sets of a sixteen octavo volume work. The printing was begun

at St Omers, but with the approach of warring armies it
was judged safer to transfer the order to Antwerp.   [198]
Fr Charles Newdigate was an expert on the press and he
calculated that in its heyday it was producing almost as
many books as all other Catholic presses put together. The
St Omers press followed the fortunes of the neighbouring
English College and flourished until 1635. In that year the
Thirty Years War came near and study had to stop for a
month while the boys helped repair the city ramparts.
Two years later St Omers was under siege by a French
army and in 1644 the Civil War was under way in
England. Many senior boys returned to fight for the King.
It became increasingly hard to make the Channel crossing
and numbers at the college fell to twenty-four. The press
went out of business in 1642; it produced no more books
until 1671.   [199]
Now we must turn to the authors. The priests of the day
were so familiar with Latin that the art of writing English
was a novelty. Those who had this fluency were busy with
their pens. Henry More, Michael Walpole, Thomas   [200]
Fitzherbert, John Salisbury and Thomas Everard were
among them. Everard for preference translated the great
spiritual classics of Albert the Great, Canisius, Bellarmine
and Borgia. By 1610 the correspondents from England
could report that King James I had read Bellarmine's book
while considerable good had been done by Francis Walsingham's *History of the Conversion of a Gentleman.* He had
written his *Search into matters of religion* in 1609 while a
student in Rome at the English College at the advanced
age of thirty-two. He had been student, soldier and lawyer
and was a relation, probably a nephew, of Elizabeth's
Secretary of State.   [201]
The *Annual Letters* often refer to recusant publications.
Their productions in pamphlet form, written in the
vernacular tongue, were circulated throughout England
with happy results. They effect what could scarcely be
done by priests, for to persuade a Protestant to forsake his
sect and be reconciled to the Church was a capital offence.

It was then difficult and dangerous to talk to them about religion, but nothing was easier than to call their attention [202] to a new book which they eagerly devoured.

The distribution of books proved a difficult and a dangerous task. Government spies were very interested in St Omers and in 1622 Henry Taylor, a Catholic printer, warned the rector of Douai against a Mr Floyd who had furnished the King of England's agent with a list of all the Catholic books printed there in English these last six years. To his credit, John Gee makes no effort to disguise papist success: he writes 'that I verily believe they have vented more of their pamphlets in this twelve months than they did in many years before [1624].'

John Percy is a Jesuit who takes us back to John Gerard's missionary years. A Durham man, he fled to Rheims and became a seminary priest and then a Jesuit. He was captured and found himself in the Bridewell prison at the [203] time Gerard, Lilie and Emerson were in the Clink. Gerard began by writing to Percy. Knowing this, one is less surprised to find Percy escaping by rope across the roofs of Bridewell along with seven laymen and two other priests. Once free he went to his native Durham and Richard Holtby for two years, then coming south and joining John Gerard who loved him dearly.

In and out of jails on many occasions, during confinement he debated before the Duke of Buckingham himself. The Countess became a Catholic and Percy's most generous patron. A debate was arranged between the imprisoned Jesuit and a certain Dr Fealty, probably in 1623. The poor doctor was allowed little time to deploy his arguments. Old King James took his place, on the following day sending nine pertinent questions to Percy. He answered the questions within a month. He did not act unaided and King James' nine points lead us to the brain behind the St Omers' publications. It was owned by the shrewd desiccated theologian Fr John Floyd. One cannot mention Fr Floyd without one observation. The men of the seventeenth century had to seek their salvation in their own peculiar world. Medieval men revelled in scholastic disputations. The men of the seventeenth century found their outlet in the polemical tract. A violent exchange of rude pamphlets seemed to them essential for the honour of the cause. [204]

On the Jesuit side, behind Percy, Knott and Walsingham, the popular protagonists, was the shrewd caustic spirit of John Floyd. The reality of such a paper battle is adequately proved. In 1610 the *Annual Letters* announce that the heretics prosper with their College for writers against His Holiness and the Catholic religion, and have expended 80,000 scudi in its foundation. James I planned a college of controversy in Chelsea and the secular priests [205] at Douai opened a small house of writers at Arras. Dr Richard Smith was one of the first on the staff. He owed this to his polemical skill and his friendship with Richelieu, his patron.

The Jesuits were not left behind. When their College was opened at Louvain in 1614 Acquaviva was persuaded formally to accept the wishes of the founder for a college where missionaries of the Society could be educated and writers may be retained to refute the books published by heretics, and which may be transferred to England when that country returns to the obedience of the Holy See. Thus the College at Louvain, later moved for security to Liège, had as a primary purpose the defence of the Catholic cause by the written word. Floyd had twenty-three books to his credit while he wrote under four or five aliases. He was [206] undoubtedly difficult but the Jesuit authorities always trusted him. In 1635, in a moment of crisis Fr Vitelleschi proposed that he should give all his attention to polemics and abandon any other work. He was deeply attached to Edward Knott and these two friends touched off the most heated quarrel of the age.

Dr Kellison of Douai dealt the first blow with his *Treatize on the Church and Divers Orders of the Church* in 1629, a sturdy defence of bishops with adroit digs at regulars: regulars had no place in the hierarchic government of the Church. Knott, still a prisoner in the Clink answered the good doctor, stating in the preface that he had been asked to do so and expressing dislike of such controversy. His *Modest Brief Discussion* (1630) appeared under the pseudonym of Nicholas Smith. It stirred up an international row. Floyd's *An Apology for the Holy See* [207]   caused a further outcry and was condemned by the French bishops. Even the French Jesuits were said to have disowned it. Floyd was neither afraid nor contrite. He was [208]   never condemned and the Jesuit authorities retained their trust in him. In 1633 Pope Urban VIII imposed a ban on all the contestants after which the General forbade his subjects to write on this subject.

Knott was appointed Provincial in 1639 and a group of Catholics sought to have the appointment revoked. The General refused. Knott was aware of the campaign against him and named his adversaries to the papal representative, George Con, who himself asserted that Knott was one of the most learned and prudent men in England, but no [208]   such tribute could silence Knott's enemies. He retired to live in Flanders while Henry More as Vice Provincial administered the mission. Knott returned as Provincial in 1643. So diffident as a young man, he alone among English Jesuits twice held that post, from 1639 to 1646, and 1652 [209]   until 1656 when he died.

One last activity of the London Jesuits must be considered under the heading given to this chapter, for Tyburn gallows stood on the outskirts of London and it was through London that so many Jesuits passed to their death. The visiting of prisons to console and assist the Catholic inmates was a routine task for a century. We may recall Persons' efforts to reach Thomas Pounde in prison, Garnet's long journey to Wisbech, Weston's to visit the Tower of London to see Jasper Heywood, and Robert Jones' risk to reach Roger Cadwallador in Leominster jail.

In Elizabethan and Stuart England, conditions varied from prison to prison and from reign to reign. The Tower of London, a place of horror to Southwell or Owen, was comfortable enough for Jasper Heywood, nursed by his sister while awaiting banishment. John Percy, as we have seen, decided to remain in the New prison and Gerard was happy in the Clink. But by the time of the Oates plot, recusant prisoners were given no exclusive treatment and probably suffered more than their Elizabethan colleagues being locked up with murderers, highwaymen and [210] cutpurses in the common jail.

A great many Jesuits died in jail. Nicholas Owen was killed under torture; many of them died from misery and neglect. Thus Edward Mico perished in Newgate. In the [211] same conspiracy, Edward Turner and Thomas Mumford died in the Gatehouse. Edmund Neville was released from Newgate but died of injuries received at his arrest. Thomas Wilkinson died suddenly in Morpeth prison, Humphry Evans as a prisoner at Chester. William Bentney, an octogenerian, was allowed to linger in prison at Leicester. Perhaps he was the last of the Jesuits to die under the English penal system when he passed away in 1692.

Men of every creed rightly revere the names of those who have died for their beliefs. A particular honour is due to a man who makes a free decision and deliberately chooses the more heroic course. Yet a word of warning is needed, for in recusant history one finds a marked predilection for martyrs as though death made them more holy and devoted than others who were never asked to face the ultimate choice. Had John Gerard not made his successful escape from the Tower he would have died at Tyburn. One single slip and Robert Persons might well have been beatified: the same goes for Dr Richard Smith. It would be out of place to make distinctions between [212] Catholic martyrs, all of whom made the same choice. What may be said without challenge is that until those executed at Tyburn were tipped off the ladder, an act of conformity would have obtained instant reprieve for any one of them.

The rubrics of execution varied little across a century. Public hangings in London were a national entertainment with the London mob markedly conservative. When the Sheriffs of London were absent at the death of Thomas Holland this was noted with astonishment. The public hangman was, as often as not, a kindly, well-intentioned fellow. By tradition he always asked forgiveness, adjusted [213] the noose and took the traditional tip. The moment of death in theory was decided by the Sheriff, though in practice the priests had arranged previously for a certain sign. Normally Catholic prisoners asked for time for private prayer; the five Jesuit martyrs of the Oates plot absolved each other, while in other cases this charity was dispensed by a priest in the crowd.

If the full barbaric sentence was completed, the hangman cut the rope while the victim was still breathing and began quartering while he was still alive. With the greater number of priests the crowd rejected the full ritual [214] and insisted that the man be dead before the hangman cut the rope. In Stuart days executions were less brutal. By the reign of James I men like Francis Bacon recognized that executions for religion damaged the government. Public opinion in England was alienated and much harm done on the Continent.

In Stuart times most priests were able to offer Mass in prison the day they were to die. Two or three had their portraits painted, friends having commissioned artists. Many had a meal before they mounted the hurdle. Thomas Garnet on the day of his death was up at six o'clock, when the prison chaplain called to encourage him. A most sympathetic man, he wrote a moving account of Garnet's last days, an account that has happily survived. Michael Walpole, present at his death, estimated that about a thou-[215] sand people witnessed it.

Despite diversions, the public execution demanded of the condemned man a terrifying toll. Yet such was the desire of so many priests to die that most met the final crisis with astonishing calm. Asked on the scaffold in Glasgow was he afraid to die, John Ogilvie gave answer no more than you are of the dishes when you go to supper.

Ogilvie cherished the hope of martydom from boyhood. Working in Edinburgh and Glasgow, strongholds of the Kirk, he celebrated Mass in both cities, drew many [216] Catholics to him and asked no mercy after capture. Two Jesuits, Francis Page and Ralph Corby, suffered spiritual distress initially when faced with the prospect of death, but both recovered when it came to it.

Peter Wright's was possibly the first martyrdom [217] reported in the press. He was described as an excellent [218] man, of firm and undaunted courage who was hung in defence of his religion and his body quartered. Wright was indeed an excellent man. He was born in 1603 in the parish of Slipton in Northamptonshire, one of thirteen children of devout recusant parents. He worked for ten years as a clerk in an attorney's office, almost abandoned his faith and, when his plan to marry a wealthy young lady living in the attorney's house was thwarted by the latter, he enlisted for service in the Dutch war in 1627 or 1628.

Worried about his faith, and disliking the army and its licentiousness he openly deserted, and boarded a boat under fire from his comrades. He wandered aimlessly in Spanish Flanders, was robbed of his few possessions and ended up at the English College in Liège. After two years of study, he entered the Society, and proved a good scholar but showed no aptitude at St Omers, in supervis- [219] ing little boys. His break came when he was sent as an army chaplain to serve the English and Irish soldiers in Flanders under Colonel Sir Harry Gage, a devout Catholic who became Wright's intimate friend. They served seven years in Flanders and returned together at the outbreak of the Civil War. Wright was with Gage when the latter raised the siege of Basing House. There Wright met the Marquis of Winchester, a Catholic and his friend and patron for many years. Wright was with Gage when he fell in a skirmish at Abingdon, and gave him the last sacraments.

After the war he lived in London, a dangerous assignment, for the city was in the hands of the Puritans. The

Jesuit lodged with the Marquis of Winchester but served the Catholics in many parts of London. He was captured in the Marquis's house, probably on the Feast of the Purification, in 1650. Wright was about to offer Mass. He attempted to escape across the roof but was captured among the chimneys, and taken below as a prisoner to the Marquis's room. There the whole family bade him adieu, with very great respect and sorrow, though they did not disclose he was a priest. The same family, a year later, would appear on the balcony to greet him as he passed on the hurdle to his death. Wright almost escaped the gallows, for the authorities of the new republic were reluc-
[220] tant to hang a man for being a priest. At his trial was a witness, Thomas Gage, a renegade priest, the brother of Sir Henry Gage who also had two brothers who were priests, one a Jesuit. Wright was regretfully condemned, but a reprieve was expected every minute; alas in the new republic few dared to act without the permission of Parliament, and it was at that time enjoying its Whitsun recess.

A multitude flocked to this great spectacle, rather a triumphal procession than of one going to execution, bearing more the appearance of rejoicing than of grief. The pious boldness of the Catholics enhanced the triumph of
[221] the victor. At the place of execution he found himself assisted in rising from the sledge by Fr Edward Latham, a
[222] man most dear to him of all the Society, and a quondam brother in the Camp mission in Belgium. He was dressed in a hempen frock, disguised as a common hodman, and in his eagerness to console his companion he was careless of his own life, but was at once recognized by Fr Peter. And indeed, on which ever side the martyr turned his
[223] eyes, his fellow religious so surrounded the gallows that he found others ready to give him absolution.

After the priest had been hanged and quartered, the London Sheriff demanded in a loud voice, with a humanity wholly unheard of, if there were any friends of the noble gentleman present. They were welcome to take the head and members and bury them with all the honour they wished. They did, returning them for burial to the Provincial. The body was shipped to St Omers to be buried there. A Member of Parliament commented that the papists were absurdly worshipping their dead priest, but we have [223] acted much more absurdly in condemning such a man to death.

8

The end of the Stuarts

The year 1680 marked the centenaries of the Jesuits' arrival in England and the publication of Campion's *Brag*. Both centenaries passed unnoticed. The Popish plot was at its peak and so many Catholics lay in prison that they could not cope with any more. The Popish Plot was revealed to the Privy Council by Titus Oates in September 1678. For a full five months after this the English Jesuits overseas had no direct news of their colleagues in England beyond the fact that the Provincial Thomas Whitbread, his secretary Edward Mico, and the procurator William Ireland and a [225] great many other Jesuits were in jail.

The General asked Fr John Warner, rector of Liège, to act as Provincial and ordered that no other Jesuits should be sent to England. Warner had no news to go by except that supplied by unreliable English broadsheets and the tales of confused fugitives. Cut off from England, his chief concern was lack of money; the bursar at St Omers found it difficult to feed the boys. The first letters from England were obscure and depressing: more than thirty-six of the Fathers dead or in prison. The final toll was far heavier than this: eight more died on the scaffold and thirteen others in jail. By Easter 1679 the first panic had subsided and in June a courageous party of boys from St Omers set out for England to appear at the trial of five Jesuits as witnesses for the defence. With them went Fr Nicholas

Blundell, Francis Hildersley a Jesuit student, and Brs John
Joseph and Peter Carpenter, all of whom would swear that
Titus Oates was at St Omers when he claimed to be attending a Jesuit 'consult' in the Strand.   [226]
The Jesuits in England were reorganizing their mission
with remarkable resilience meanwhile. They held a secret
meeting, though rewards as high as four and even eight
hundred scudi were on their heads. A Protestant commen-
tator noted that 'the Jesuits fear neither death nor danger:
hang as many as you will, others are ready to take their
places.' Though the centenary of Campion's *Brag* had not
been honoured, at least his spirit was very much alive.   [227]
One may note that there were 126 Jesuits in England at the
start of the Oates plot and 92 at the close. Warner could tell
the General that whereas ten boys from St Omers would
normally apply to join the Jesuits each year, twenty had
now come forward. The noviciate at Watten could not
hold them and four would make their years of probation
in other provinces.

John Warner became the new Provincial and when the
story of that plot could be pieced together he was commissioned to make the attempt. The *History of the English
Persecution of Catholics and the Presbyterian Plot* survived to
be published in England in 1953. Warner had been born in   [228]
Warwickshire in 1628, studied in Spain, was invited to
Douai College to profess theology for four years, decided
to become a Jesuit in 1662 and soon enjoyed a high reputation in the Society. After his Provincialate was over he
was an excellent rector of St Omers before being chosen as
confessor by James II. He was devoted to Edward Petre,
and critical of John Keynes, who was to succeed him as
Provincial, and he was a sincere admirer of James II.

One cannot read Warner without facing the fact that the
Jesuits whom Charles allowed to die as traitors were
among the most loyal friends the Stuarts ever had. Warner   [229]
traces the Oates plot back to its two sources, independent
of each other and seeking different ends. First the political
force, an insane desire for revolution. He shows us

Shaftesbury was still a Cromwellian at heart, organizing at every level not to hurt Catholics, but to topple the King. Destruction of the absolute monarchy was the main aim. The Whigs' political theory was that the papists in Parliament must either be eliminated or given absolute equality. They could not destroy the monarchy while so large a minority depended on the King. Shaftesbury decided to destroy them and the Popish Plot served him as a gambit in this. The plot, raised in the first instance against the Jesuits alone, caught up all the other Catholics, the Protestants, York and the Queen, was in fact only a weapon [230] against King Charles himself.

That the Oates plot involved the Jesuits first was due to a faction inside the Catholic community. The Jesuits were more orthodox, more Roman, more unpopular, more heresy hunting since their continental battles with the Jansenists. They were also more isolated, dependent on the pope and the absolute monarchs. They were still, I believe, disciplined, sincere, pious and devoted, but naive. We know that as early as 1647 a group of Catholics had made an effort to come to terms with the Roundheads, on the basis of tolerance for papists in return for an oath of [231] allegiance that would exclude the Jesuits. Soon after the Restoration a second attempt was made to buy toleration with an oath of allegiance that no Jesuit could accept. The prime mover was Dr John Serjeant, a talented secular priest, author and theologian, a spiritual Whig with a pathological hatred of Jesuits. The Oates plot was dished up by Shaftesbury for the King's discomfort and by Serjeant to rid England of the Jesuits and as a result of it several hundred innocent people were to die.

The one hundred and thirty Jesuits who lay hiding in England knew next to nothing of these intrigues. Only when the Civil War was ended could the picture of Jesuit activities be pieced together. We hear of Fr John Falkner, at the siege of Wardour Castle in 1643, who was Chaplain to [232] the intrepid Lady Arundel. He offered Mass daily during the siege, and buried old Sir Walter who was killed in a sally. Falkner drove to Shaftesbury in Lady Arundel's carriage, leaving the castle in enemy hands. Further to the west we meet an unnamed Jesuit, a cavalry chaplain, serving in the battles of Bristol, Gloucester and Newburgh.

At least one future Jesuit saw service as a soldier. [233] William Carlos was born in Brerewood in Staffordshire, his father being the Governor of Tonge Castle. It was taken and Carlos was imprisoned then banished, the twelve-year-old William living with his mother in Brerewood until he was eighteen. His father secretly returned to England and they joined the Scottish army of King Charles II at Worcester. They were separated in the battle and William made for London where he lived until he was twenty-four. He witnessed the execution of John South-worth and he decided to go to Rome to offer himself for the priesthood, entered the Society and was to die in 1659.

After the restoration of the monarchy in 1660 the Jesuits had still suffered from the latent hostility of their enemies. The King's desire for toleration was used against them [234] through further attempts at an oath of allegiance they could not accept. The complaint that they were blocking the appointment of bishops was almost certainly unfounded. The Catholic Whigs, lead by Drs Holden and Serjeant, were in fact demanding conditions Rome would never accept. Much of this mischief-making was blamed on the Chancellor, Lord Clarendon. The Jesuits were forced to live in splendid isolation, perhaps a little complacent. Scarcely ever in the memory of the Fathers did a more joyful day dawn, than when Charles Stuart had been proclaimed King in 1660. The Jesuits were happy and [235] they were flattered when the Chancellor Clarendon showed kindness to them. Meanwhile behind the scenes they were busy for some years trying to put their own house in order, for a certain laxity had followed on the wake of war, not only in the Society but in the Catholic clergy as a whole, and the promise of toleration had drawn to London undesirable clerics of every sort. Even the easy-going King had objected.

Throughout the century of persecution General after General wrote regularly to Superiors, dealing rarely with grave matters, but mainly with minor points of discipline. Worries about the decline of Greek studies at St Omers; a professor at Liège holding strange views; an English Jesuit [236] smoking in public and playing cards for money. These letters mirror an almost morbid fascination with the Court. The General becomes excited at the news that the English monarch is to marry a Portugese princess. The Provincial in England is also excited. One may easily understand the angry attitude to Jesuits of a Dr Sergeant, who wanted to hurt them but could not, because of their [237] royal friends.

The great man the Jesuits most assiduously attended was James Duke of York. As far as is known they played no direct part in his decision to become a Catholic. He had long been attracted to the Church. His parents were very devout; his father as near a Catholic as could be, his French mother militantly so. Both Charles and James had many dealings with English Jesuits in Flanders. He was still an Anglican on the Restoration in 1660; not until 1669 did he reach his decision: he made it fully aware of the risks involved. Once it was made he rejected the [238] subterfuge of attending the Royal Chapel occasionally.

In the years before the Oates plot the situation for Catholics was therefore obscure. The King himself quite openly favoured religious toleration and though his efforts were thwarted by Parliament and the faction, these could not prevent the general relaxation of the [239] Penal Laws. Despite outward toleration and calm – [240] unknown throughout a century – many Jesuits seem to have guessed that trouble was brewing. Warner recalls the rumours spread after the fire of London, which were blaming this on the Duke of York, and on the Catholics generally, chiefly on the Jesuits. Shaftesbury and his faction were at work in this gradual building up of hysteria. Early in 1676 the new Jesuit Provincial, Thomas Whitbread, made his visitation of the College at Liège.

Addressing the community according to custom, he took as his text Christ's question to the Zebedees, can you drink the chalice I am about to drink? He put the question, were they prepared for the loss of their good name and to be accused of sedition, conspiracy against the King and wanting to overthrow the State. His words were prophetic and he himself would be in Newgate within [241] three months.

When Whitbread praised the spirit of the students at Liège, his commendations were not merely formal. The lassitude noted at the time of the Restoration had been corrected over eighteen years. The vocations from St Omers were strengthened when a number of middle-aged men of high position decided to enter the Society. John Warner was a professor from Douai; Sir Thomas Preston had been twice married before he entered the noviciate at Watten in 1674. Laurence Ireland of Lydiate had also been married but he gladly left his two little daughters in the care of his mother and crossed to Watten in 1664. Two military men became Jesuits at about this time: Charles Duke who had served in Turenne's army and Thomas Eccleston, who became a Jesuit in sorrow, having killed an adversary in a duel.

The Warner family, Suffolk folk of high social standing, were the most remarkable of these late vocations. Sir John [242] and Lady Warner, friends of Fr Travers a Jesuit, became Catholics in 1664. Lady Warner and Miss Elizabeth Warner, Sir John's sister, became religious. The whole family disposed of their possessions and the ladies left for Dover. They took with them Lady Warner's two little daughters who were left for schooling with English nuns at Dunkirk, to become nuns themselves in due course. Sir John, changing his surname to Clare, went to Watten to be a Jesuit, and his wife and sister entered the Poor Clares. John's heir and brother Francis visited him, decided to be a Carthusian but was drowned when sailing back to England in bad weather to wind up his affairs. Brother Clare, SJ was given the privilege by the General of pronouncing his vows in the Poor Clares' chapel on the same day as his wife took hers. Sir John became Provincial [243] of the Jesuits in 1689.

Bathos is unavoidable because we pass now to the oddest and most disreputable of Jesuit aspirants: Titus Oates presented himself as a candidate in 1677 at the English College, Valladolid. As a servant at a Cambridge college he was sacked for stealing, jailed for perjury at Hastings, obtained a rectory at Bobing from which he was discharged for his disreputable life, became a Catholic and approached the Jesuits who, zealous to help everyone, sent him to Valladolid. Oates was returned as unsuitable but Fr Strange, the Provincial, sent him to St Omers. Fr Strange was mild and ineffectual as Provincial though something of a scholar. Oates fooled him. The cunning, traditional to Jesuits, was not here displayed. He stayed at the College from December 1677 to June 1678 when the new Provincial Fr Whitbread sent him packing for misde- [244] meanours and treasonable words.

He certainly never attended the notorious Consult in [245] London 24th–26th April 1678. Such Congregations were limited to the forty senior Fathers and some Superiors. Oates had no place there. At St Omers he was a guest; he had not been accepted as a novice. The Congregation was a routine meeting held every three years to elect a procu- rator to represent the Province in Rome. Oates may have heard a little general gossip, none it of any value; because the business of a Provincial Congregation is never discussed publicly. The meeting was routine; the details of [245] it have been published. Foley prints Oates's original reve- lations as they were put before the King, and the Privy Council, many of whom must have known them to be false. Charles tripped the perjurer up, but the biggest of his lies could not be contradicted. The Consult had been held, not as Oates had said in the White Horse Inn in the Strand but in St James's Palace, in the Duke of York's rooms. It was not easy for Jesuits to find a suitable meeting for forty Fathers. The household of the Duke of York made a gesture which the Jesuits accepted without a thought about risk. The King said nothing and the Duke said [246] nothing when Oates swore he had attended the Consult in the Strand. The Jesuits kept silent so as not to embarrass their royal friend.

Oates, as the saviour of the nation, was allowed to set out on his nightly rounds, flanked by his bodyguard of thugs. Anyone whom he cared to name was arrested as a traitor. One of the first to receive a visit was the Jesuit Provincial, Thomas Whitbread, who had expelled Oates from St Omers three months before. The arrests went on for days and with them a crop of rumours deliberately spread. London was hysterical with yarns about thousands of Irishmen and Frenchmen crouching in their cellars ready, at a signal, to leap out and slit all honest Protestant throats. A vast anti-Catholic parade wound its way through the city. The picture given by all is one of cruelty, suffering and terror. If so much as a popish dog or cat had appeared in the streets, wrote one observer, it would have been torn to pieces immediately. [247]

The Jesuits later reported that in the opening stages of the assault hostility was mainly directed against their body and that a group of Catholics gave their approval to this purge. Dr Serjeant earned a mention in the *Annual Letters:* he and another priest David Maurice became informers in close communion with the Privy Council and spread abroad a report that the English Province of the Society was at an end, that the martyrs had been justly convicted for high treason. Serjeant remained a practising priest, continued to attend Chapter meetings, and enjoyed a fine funeral paid for by the Chapter when he died in 1707. Today we know that the treachery may have reached back to 1671. [248]

Two men seem to have known the full story; Malcolm Hay who in our century fitted the clues together and Fr John Warner, in 1684. Warner could sum up the case of Dr [249] Serjeant thus: 'I should not readily allow myself to be persuaded that Serjeant communicated his designs to his fellow seculars and far less that they approved of them. Rather I am convinced that Serjeant himself now condemns them.' Had not Malcom Hay re-opened the

[250] scandal of Dr Serjeant, these discreditable facts might have remained interred. Hay wrote in the spirit of a skilled historian. His grievance was directed first to Whig historians – Winston Churchill among them – who without documentary evidence told and retold unproven tales.

Hay tells us that since the middle of the seventeenth century down to the present day, misrepresentations have pursued the Jesuits even to the dictionary. They have been judicially reprimanded by Hallam, elegantly reproved by Macaulay, sorrowfully condemned by Manning: lesser celebrities have faithfully followed the train. And it is indeed strange that Dr John Serjeant, the energetic pioneer who started the campaign should ungratefully, though

[251] conveniently, have been forgotten.

The sufferings caused by Titus Oates to hundreds of innocent people were unmerited and severe. While the Gunpowder Plot was possibly government sponsored, here there was no plot of any kind. Of the Jesuits who died at Tyburn none was in any way distinguished save in bravery and innocence. Fr Alexander Keynes went to Tyburn to watch his five Jesuit colleagues die. He says that before they arrived he felt somewhat downhearted but as soon as he saw these noble champions of Christ the sight dispelled his fears. During the whole time they were engaged in their address to the people and their devotions, the stillness and silence of the surrounding multitudes struck him as wonderful. He heard no insult-

[252] ing voice raised.

For eighteen months the Jesuits in every part of the country were on the run. Peter Hamerton successfully passed the trained bands guarding the bridge at Doncaster, Charles Poulton spent much of the winter hiding in woods and thickets, Alexander Keynes acquired a passport and made for the Continent. Michael Aylworth got away to Holland to die of his sufferings endured in the

Derbyshire district in 1679. In Wales two Jesuits were [253]
caught and hanged. David Lewis was captured on 17th
November 1678. John Evans was hanged in Cardiff; Lewis,
who left behind an account of his suffering, was executed
at Usk. Hundreds of innocent people died through the
Oates plot: one Jesuit, William Culcheth, reckoned four
hundred did so in prison. King Charles, knowing full well
the plot was a fraud, made no effort to stop it. The Jesuits
saw his dilemma, for Charles could have stood for justice
only at the cost of civil war. In the end he defeated Shaftes- [254]
bury. After years of temporizing he died a Catholic.

The throne which the double-jointed Charles held for
twenty-five years was lost by his brother in three.
Absolute monarchy was probably doomed with the execution of Charles I. No modern Jesuit need mourn its passing
but may well regret the methods used. King Charles was
scarcely more honourable than his adversaries. No Jesuit
had much reason to love the Stuarts, so often treacherous
in practice, though noble in intent. The Stuarts however
seem noble when set beside Shaftesbury and his Whigs.
Shaftesbury's use of propaganda was as clever as any seen
in later centuries. He stands as the architect of the revolution, so quaintly named Glorious. [255]

The new king enjoyed wide experience, much of it
painful: his father's execution, the years of exile, during
which he served as a soldier with courage and success. His
career as an admiral had been distinguished. His heart
and soul were set on the flourishing of the navy. Nor did
James show himself in Scotland as wanting in diplomacy
or tact. How far must one travel forwards or backwards
through the list of English monarchs to find another with
equal accomplishments? He was also a deeply religious
man. A pious king is not necessarily a good king but he [256]
stands a good chance of proving himself an honourable
one.

It seemed unlikely that prayer alone would solve the
problems inherited from his brother, not least the mounting antipathy for France. On the accession of the new king,

Jesuits were at first cautious. They report his open profession of faith. An astonishing increase in the number of open Catholics lead the Provincial to fill the gaps left by the plot, combing Flanders for suitable men. The king wished to see his own religion embraced but thought it contrary to Holy writ to force conscience. At no time did [256] he intend to impose Catholicism by force.

[257]   Two questions come to mind in reading the story of James II. Did he expect to keep his throne or want to keep it? Would he have behaved differently had his son been born earlier in his reign? The Jesuits were not unaware of the mounting opposition, many of the upper classes and the army turning against their lawful monarch, a rebellion more impelled by the hatred of the faith, than attachment [258] to their own sect. For three years the Jesuits worked openly and successfully, their first and only opportunity in a hundred years. Success came too late, for they started to see results in the very year that all would be swept away.

Churches were seen to rise in principal cities, great numbers assembled everywhere to receive the sacraments and in various areas free schools were established in which not only Catholics but also Protestants were instructed in humanity studies and good morals. The Fathers visited towns and villages everywhere, confirming those who had held the faith and bringing back Protestants to the fold of Christ. How far all this was wishful thinking was hard to say. Much local evidence survives of remarkable expansion. If in every part of England the efforts of the Jesuits were unsparing, in [259] London these received most complete success.

For the first time in a century a Jesuit house was opened in England to be run in the style common on the Continent. A site for a school was purchased near the Savoy. Building began in January 1687 and the community [260] moved in in May. The College opened in 1687 and two hundred and fifty boys presented themselves on the opening day. Education would be free, and Catholic and non-Catholic boys would be admitted; the latter would not be expected to change their beliefs. Inside the short space of three years the Jesuits had opened another school in the very heart of London in a building attached to the Bavarian embassy. The chapel here had first been served by secular priests but was handed over to the Jesuits in 1688 on the King's orders. [261]

Fr Edward Petre was one of the few nationally famous Jesuits, second only to Robert Persons in unpopularity. Yet the case of Edward Petre proves more baffling than his. Persons was a brilliant man with a policy that provoked conflict. Petre was a dull man with a public career covering not more than three years. Two of his brothers were Jesuits, two of his sisters nuns. Edward became a Jesuit in 1652, was successful in his studies and professed in 1671. Succeeding to the baronetcy, he returned to England sometime before the discovery of the Oates plot in 1678 when he was imprisoned, being released on bail in 1683. Proposed for the office of Provincial, John Keynes was in fact chosen. Petre went to St Omers, was appointed rector [262] and glowing reports of his work were sent to Rome. A letter of thanks was sent to him and to his community at St Omers, for the kindness shown to an Irish regiment quartered in that town. He died at Watten at the age of sixty-eight. [263]

Petre was a capable, popular harmless man universally decried as a villain during three out of sixty-eight years of his life. Some of the charges against him may be brushed aside as vicious and ridiculous; they included black magic, being the true father of the baby smuggled into the Queen's bed in a warming pan and having got away with £60,000 packed in several great chests. But a number of honourable men also blamed him for their plight. It is not known when James, Duke of York first made friends with Edward Petre but a hint is given in the Jesuit papers that the Duke saved Petre from the gallows in the Popish plot.

When James ascended the throne he asked the Provincial for the services of Petre, to be in charge of the Chapel

Royal. He asked to resign at least on one occasion. James
sent a message to the Pope that he knew not where to find
another so diligent, faithful and well versed in the affairs
he confides in him. After he had fled abroad the King
dispelled all calumnies raised against the Father by
publicly declaring that had he but listened to Fr Petre's
Councils his affairs would have been in a very different
[265] position. One fact may be established beyond dispute, Fr
Petre was an amateur in politics.

Why he ever went to Court, or was ever allowed to go
by his superiors, is a mystery. The General showed great
reservations but at the end followed the English Provincial's advice. In January 1688, the General expresses
surprise to the Provincial that Fr Petre has been given a
seat in the Privy Council without his being informed. The
Provincial must take responsibility for the promotion for
reasons we may guess. At the head comes the King's
persistence: he would not take no for an answer in seeking
to get him a cardinal's hat, a promotion rejected by the
Pope, disliked by the General and according to the King,
never sought by Petre himself. The whole incident is extraordinary.

The King, who was negotiating for the appointment of
Vicars Apostolic, must have known very well the likely
resentment of many secular clergy were a Jesuit to be
made a cardinal. Petre we know was charged in Rome
with ambition when the Society was much on the defen-
sive and the first faint rumours were in circulation that the
Order would be suppressed. This much good came of the
whole attempt, that the King, the Provincial the General
and the Pope all expressed their conviction of Petre's innocence.

The English Provincial was weak, unable to resist a
monarch who had shown such affection for the English
Jesuits. Petre played no important role at Court, kept clear
of politics and may well have exercised a restraining
[266] influence. With so much of the pretended evidence
weighted against him by those planning a revolution or, in

failure, looking for a scapegoat, it seems likely that Fr
Petre made no fatal mistake beyond the first one of accepting a position at Court. With so many enemies watching
his every move, it redounds greatly to his credit that so
little of substance could be levelled against his name. The
Whig historians would later release much abuse against
him as a man of no learning or anyway famed for virtue;
Lord Macauley summed up for the Whigs, saying that of
all the evil counsellors who had access to the royal ear, he
perhaps bore the largest part in the ruin of the house of
Stuart. The philosopher Leibniz, tells a different story. Fr
Petre, with the tide in his favour showed moderation; it
was not he who urged the King to his rash counsels.   [267]
    With one final piece of Whig reporting we may leave Fr
Petre for good. One of the tasks to which he was assigned   [268]
included a genuine effort towards liberty of conscience for
nonconformists of every type. In this, King James was well
in advance of his time, and both Petre and Warner played
some part in it. No credit was given them. Indeed after
James had fled and Petre was in disgrace Gee published an
edition of Robert Persons' *Memorial* to whip up animosity
to the Jesuits. The fall of King James is told in every textbook. The Jesuit version enjoys one advantage: they were
in no way taken by surprise. They knew well the Glorious
Revolution was contrived. The rumours of the intended
invasion reached London long before William of Orange
had embarked. The sudden increase of lampoons, the wild
crop of terrifying rumours, were clear signs to those who
had suffered in the Oates plot. People became more auda-   [269]
cious, rose up against the Catholics and attacked them.
The blasphemies, the lies, abuse, bawdy songs and libel-
lous tracts that preceded Orange fill any decent man with
shame. The old, old story was put about that French and
Irish soldiers were lurking in every cellar to cut honest
Protestant throats.
    Devotion to King James survived aggressively for half a
century. The doubts about the birth of a son were raised
later; at the time the country heard the news with at least

[270]   public delight. Some fifty distinguished people were present and witnesses to the birth. The baby prince was baptized the next day. The birth was publicly attested. Yet to the faction the event was inconvenient and had to be challenged at once. So came the warming pan with the bawdy attempts to guess the father; chief candidates were Petre and the papal nuncio. The fury of the mob turned against the Jesuit College in the city, was uncontrolled and broke loose against all Catholics and sacred edifices.

The Jesuits were compelled to hide or fly. Twenty were captured and imprisoned. They never deserted King James and he in exile never lost his affection for them. When he died, Louis XIV insisted on a full state burial. [271]   Parts of his body were deposited in different churches; the remains were buried at the English College at St Omers. Meanwhile the Jesuits were resilient. The annual letters for 1695 aver that heaven never shone more benignly upon the English College of Liège than in the past year. Lord Blackwaite, the secretary to the Prince of Orange, in a letter addressed to a priest at the College, returned thanks in the name of the Prince for charity shown to sick [272]   soldiers.

9

Who joined the Jesuits and why

By the start of the eighteenth century, the popular image of the English Jesuit had taken shape. The very word was alarming, expressing all that was most shifty in the Church of Rome. That Jesuits were utterly devoted – Lord Macauley's admission – made them doubly dangerous. Jesuits practised equivocation, permitted the killing of kings, pledged themselves to foreign monarchs, proclaimed the immoral doctrine that the end justifies the means. Hallam could find no proof of Campion's treason but his being a Jesuit rendered it probable. Elizabethans whispered excitedly when a Jesuit was captured. John Worthington found that they thought him to be a great man of note. At Tyburn Jesuits, at the end, disclosed their calling, to hang with extra prestige. In 1891 Professor Gardiner gladly apologized and changed a statement that Jesuits had to obey Superiors even in the matter of sin. In 1901 Fr Bernard Vaughan won his celebrated libel action on the so-called Jesuit doctrine that the end justifies the means.

Inside the Catholic community, opinions varied and the Jesuits enjoyed a triple image. The more radical of their priestly opponents accused the Fathers openly of crime. [274] More followed the line of Cardinal Manning, deploring the aristocratic, military, exclusive spirit, their contempt for their fellow priests. All these pay a backhanded tribute

to the Jesuits, admitting that they were capable, dynamic, thrusting, a force to be reckoned with. Others nearer the mark saw Jesuits as living on their sinister reputation while they were no more than average; a statement of this was made by the fictional Hadrian VII in Baron Corvo's romance. He denounced them for their false pretences, showy erudition and superficial machinations, which were silly. They were not monsters but ridiculous medioc-
[275] rities always pitifully burrowing.

The Jesuits then had their critics but they also had many friends. Most of them were the alumni of their colleges, or the innumerable converts they made. Perhaps the most extraordinary defence of the Jesuits is to be found in that most unlikely of literary hiding places, the official biography of Manning. Purcell lets fly, with the dead eminence's strictures before him, saying that the reverence and gratitude entertained by the English Catholics for the eminent services rendered to the Church in England in the present as in the past, was far too deeply seated in their hearts and minds to have been perturbed even by the persistent opposition and prejudice against them displayed by Cardinal Manning during the whole period of his episcopal rule.

How may one uncover the truth about Jesuits? They may claim one unique achievement, maintaining across four centuries with no obvious effort, four or five conflicting images. Where in history, outside the Communist parties, may one find a body which has commanded so much suspicion, affection, adulation and contempt? Two questions come to mind: where do Jesuits come from and
[276] who in his senses would volunteer to become a Jesuit?

Down to 1914 one third of Jesuits came from families such as Petre, Plowden, Constable, Maxwell, Gordon, Pole, Clifford, Arundel, Weld, Keynes, Vaughan, Tichborne, Darrell, Scarisbrick, Mainwaring, Blundell, More and the rest. If we take two or three names at random, we find that eleven Petres, ten Poles and sixteen Poultons entered the society. All these old families were greatly reduced in wealth by the annual drain of fines. A number of Jesuits inherited titles but never used them. A few did. Gilbert Talbot died as the 13th Earl of Shrews- [277] bury, Fr Molyneux became 7th viscount and so on. In the main Jesuits were classless, according to the founders plan. The point is well proved in the lives of those who died martyrs who must occupy the highest place in the Jesuit roll of honour. Only two, Southwell and Ogilvie, could claim noble connections. The others came from families of no pretensions. Campion's father was a book-seller, John Cornwell had been found as a little boy reading a book under a hedge and Sir John Arundell saw he went to Oxford, Peter Wright was a clerk, Ralph Corby's father had been agent for Lady Kildare, David Lewis and Henry Garnett were sons of schoolmasters, Edward and Anthony Turner were from a rectory, Morse, Page and Henry Walpole began as law students, Edward Oldcorne was the son of a Yorkshire bricklayer, and Ralph Ashley was a cook. [278]

In Victorian times we find the same hotch-potch. The Vaughans, the Cliffords and the Welds came from the landed gentry, but Frs Rickaby, John and Joseph were sons of a coachman and the three Fathers Bond were sons of a gardener. Fr Kerr had been a naval commander, and was of noble Scottish lineage, De Vere Beauclerk could look back to Nell Gwynne, Manley Hopkins was a pupil at a grammar school in Highgate and Fr Ernest Harper had taught physical training at the London polytechnic. It is recorded that after a fall in the street, he performed a double back lift and thus checked the enthusiasm of an oncoming cab.

The Jesuits decided their admissions neither on class or brains. A more varied group of novices could hardly have been imagined and the myth of the learned or aristocratic Jesuit may be laid for good. Richard Clarke is one of those who sounds class conscious. Huson was an American [279] medical student, Ross as a novice was still a deputy sheriff in Ireland, Dominic Thorner had studied music in Naples and conducted his own opera in Lisbon.

If we enquire why so many types reached the cold decision to join the Jesuits, certain common motives may help to answer the question. The very unpopularity of Jesuits worked in their favour, especially with converts and ardent Catholics. Thomas Garnet applied to enter the order in 1604 because of the odium heaped on it: during the Oates plot the number of those applying to join doubled. Edmund Lester was a young convert and he read an attack on them; they seemed always to be up to something dashing and daring. Stephen Webb MC and bar, who had once shifted a load of ammunition while under enemy fire, entered when 35 years old because they came in for such a large share of the world's calumny and he

[280]   wanted to share this with them. Thorner watched the Jesuits expelled from Naples and when he saw the infuriated mob escorting them conceived an admiration and love for them. Attachment to a particular Jesuit was another reason. Four of five Walpoles became Jesuits under John Gerard's gift of sympathy.

[281]   A further cause was spiritual upheaval. So many of those who became Jesuits in earlier centuries did so because of spiritual fears. After receiving the Anglican diaconate, Campion suffered guilt for years. Henry Belfield was never a heretic but fear of the plague made him more careful about religion. Sir John Warner and his whole family were much exercised by purgatory. Later as a novice Sir John had a further scruple; more than a century earlier his estate at Parham had belonged to a

[282]   monastery. Fr Thomas Poulton gave a long account of his struggles and fears before he finally arrived in Rome to enter the English College. Sixteen Poultons were to be Jesuits.

Fr John Gerard proved to be the perfect spiritual director, persuading many to make the Spiritual Exercises, knowing them to be a powerful remedy. When he designed his scheme Ignatius was himself a layman, a recent victim of such scruples and fears. Far from pooh-poohing mental distress he expected it and made allowance for it, starting his Exercises with certain basic lessons for the right ordering of one's life. Newman [285] studied the Exercises and pays tribute to the Spanish saint in his *Apologia*. What I can speak of with greater confidence, he said, is the effect produced in me by studying them. For here again, in a matter consisting in the purest and most direct acts of religion – intercourse between God and the soul, during a season of recollection, or penance, of good resolution, of inquiry into vocation – the soul was *sola cum solo*; there was no cloud interposed between the creature and the Object of his faith and love. The command practically enforced was, my son, give me thy heart. [286]

Yet not even Newman the Victorian could guess the impact of the Ignatian Exercises on men of an earlier age, the Renaissance era. Those who found peace through the Exercises tended to stay with the Jesuits. This was the case with the companions of Mary Ward. Jesuit sodalities for men were closely tied to the Exercises and the sodalists, laymen of influence and position were deeply attached to the Jesuits. How far individual Jesuits used them as a means to power is not easy to decide. This much is certain, that the Exercises were of primary importance in the fashioning of the seventeenth-century Church. [287]

To form an accurate image of the English Jesuit, the method of training has to be assessed. Novices, on entering the Society, first made the Spiritual Exercises for the full period of thirty days. This, rather than any external qualifications, served as the initial test. Academic honours were certainly not required and a working knowledge of Latin alone was indispensable. Not until the 1930s was a London matriculation spoken of as a prerequisite. Money [288] was not required for admission. Some were men of wealth and position, but many had nothing to give. The age for admission was not decided, though Ignatius wanted men not boys. Novices were usually seventeen or more, but could be much older. From 1625–1774 they came to Watten to start; the village lay two or three miles from St

Omers. The novices gave catechism lessons to local children and some learned Flemish for the purpose. All the world over Jesuit novices followed the same pattern of training for two years. At Watten they worked in the house, on the farm, or in the orchards and some took care [289] of the sick.

[290]   A regular noviciate test was a pilgrimage, made even in winter, during which they had to beg their food. The novice masters were competent rather than distinguished. A description of Watten survives, drawn up by the French when they seized it in 1764. Four rooms were set aside for a tailor's shop, infirmary and pharmacy; there was a windmill and a boat used for bringing food from St Omers; for eight months of the year the roads were impassible. Had they not worked their own farm and also had aid from England, they could not have survived. They distributed alms in a generous and charitable way.

The *Confessions of St Augustine*, Roper's *Life of St Thomas More*, Persons' *Christian Directory*, and Southwell's [no connection with the martyr] *Journal of Meditations* were the [290] staples of their spiritual and prayer lives. The novices did [291] much of their reading in French. Lallemant and Croiset were the classics of the 17th and 18th centuries. Alphonsus Rodriguez *Practice of Perfection and Christian Virtues* takes one back to the days of Teresa of Avila, and was the staple of the English noviciate at the start of the Hitler war. Jesuits were bilingual because English religious literature needed supplementing by the French. The Jesuits with so great a reputation for devilment were in fact painfully slow moving. Charles Plowden's notes of 1803 as novice master were in use a century later. In the 1930s English novices read Rodriguez in the French of Bossuet. If the novices came nervous and fearful, they left two years later impossibly sane.

After the two years, a very mixed bunch of novices took their first vows. Some had been overseas since early adolescence and knew little of the world while Peter Wright had been a soldier, Thomas Poulton a merchant, and Emmanuel

Lob had been training as one. Henry Foster, eighteen years
married and once wealthy, had been ruined by his fidelity
to religion, took vows in 1655, had two sons in the Society [292]
and six daughters became nuns. From the noviceship they
followed different routes. Edward Petre had been nineteen
years a Jesuit before his solemn profession. Robert Persons,
a century earlier, was ordained after three. In 1880 sixteen
years between entry and ordination was the norm. But
Richard Cooper, for example, was ordained after eight and
sent to India, to return later to make up his studies. Long
delays meant no lack of virtue, usually the opposite; a good
man could not be spared.

A Jesuit was a Jesuit after the noviciate and took three
vows; poverty, chastity and obedience. Many distinguished men elected not to be priests. There were no lay
Jesuits. The noviceship was common to all, the vows made
one a Jesuit for ever: after that each man followed the
direction of Superiors. Sooner or later every English Jesuit [293]
visited Liège, the Anglo-Bavarian College on a hill north
of the city, for higher studies, a rendezvous for recusants,
writers, army chaplains, Jesuit and lay students. There
was a well laid-out garden, a playing field and an orchard.
In the gardens was an unusual sundial telling not only the
hour but other secrets of geography, astrology and astron-
omy. Its inventor Fr Francis Line constructed a still more
unusual dial for King Charles II.

In 1669 Maximilian of Bavaria gave an annual pension
to the College, though in fact as we have seen the bulk of
the money for the buildings came from England. A farm at
Chevremont outside the city had a villa for holidays with
a chapel in honour of Our Lady. The Jesuits at Liège kept
to themselves, respecting the rights of the Walloon Jesuits
and avoiding the political entanglements of the town. [294]
Once or twice they were involved in civic disputes. More
peaceful crowds visited the College, many for Vespers on
Sunday evening. During bouts of the plague the students
went out to nurse the striken. The mortality rate among
young Jesuits was high at Liège, St Omers, Ghent, Watten

and the colleges of Spain. Frequent epidemics throughout Europe made old age seem a miracle. The Jesuits met the [295] threat with the confraternity of a happy death, which they borrowed from their Continental colleagues. Every month, on the first Sunday, special prayers and litanies were said. In Liège, as in all their houses, it was an unqualified success. They brought the *Bona Mors Confraternity* to England and, until the Second World War, the Confraternity with its monthly prayers flourished at Stonyhurst, Wimbledon and Farm Street. Medical science has improved, and anxiety about a happy death has gone.

The full course at Liège covered six or seven years of philosophy and theology. There was no trace of learning, deceit or intrigue in this; the English Jesuit professors [296] were sober, dull, post-Tridentine. To be fair we must remember that those in exile are greatly handicapped in scholarship, with inaccessibility of historical sources and the shortage of books. Further the professors were training their men, not to be scholars, but to be active apostles in a dangerous mission field. Constant attention to refuting heretics produced a negative form of scholarship. Two years at Watten, then seven years at Liège must have seemed a long apprenticeship for students with their heart on their native land.

The students went weekly to Chrevemont for recreation and also enjoyed a summer break. Rarely if ever were they able to return home during their years of study. We have details of special novenas, fastdays, the annual retreat, austerities, litany of the Saints recited each day, penances in the refectory. A touching complacency is seen in the solemn inclusion in the *Annual Letters*, of compliments paid by visitors. These young Jesuits speak for themselves only on rare occasions.

One of the most sensational of these was provoked in 1640, by the Provincial Fr Edward Knott. The Maryland mission was six years old, Andrew White and his companions were living in pitiful conditions and the Provincial sent a letter to the Continental houses asking for volunteers. The response was immediate. The young seminarians preparing for ordination were all anxious to go. Some write with [297] hilarity, others only after considerable thought. Francis Parker's offer was a result of his hope one day to return to England to bring his family back to the faith. John Parker, a namesake, thought that he would be unacceptable because of ill health, but assured the Provincial he was better. Laurence Worsley simply started by claiming there was none fitter or of better will than he. Fr Christopher, a [298] professor and reputed to know eleven languages, thought this facility might be useful. There were many others. Sadly none of those here quoted were sent.

In Persons' day the principal aim was to send priests to [299] England, but after the Restoration only those could work there for whom shelter and protection could be found. The urgency was fading, the number of family chaplaincies was declining, and only those who could adjust to the vagaries of eighteenth-century rural life were sent to England. The reign of James II was exceptional and many Jesuits were needed for the colleges and parishes that were rising, but with his fall, the pattern of Catholic life in England changed. More mature priests were sent to England there to remain. Many·younger priests remained out of England for many years.

In 1693 of 119 who worked in England, all but three were priests. The Continental colleges were manned by 155 priests, brothers, students. Another forty were scattered through Europe. Ten staffed the mission in Maryland. As the decades passed, the College of St Omers could be seen as the most enduring of Persons' schemes. Though England and France were at war for most of a century, recusant children still reached colleges overseas. [300] Despite all the ups and downs, a secret ceaseless traffic was maintained over two centuries, though St Omers could not have survived without royal pensions, first from Philip II of Spain, later from Louis XIV, after the town fell to the French in 1680. With such outside help the fees could be kept within reason. [301]

For many young Jesuits, work at this College became a life career. They came to St Omers as boys or older men, next they were trained here in Jesuit pedagogic methods; finally, after ordination they might be posted to St Omers as members of the staff. Not all Jesuits were successful in the classroom. Peter Wright found that nothing could be less consonant with his natural inclinations than this trying office. John Warner, as rector of St Omers found a certain Fr Janion impossible. A sociable man, he joined the boys at their games and talked to them without limit: a powerful young man he would also show off by lifting weights. Janion was posted as a camp missioner in Flanders. Other Jesuits loved their work and were much loved by their pupils. Charles Wharton, who left the Society and the Church, kept a deep affection for Fr Walsh, his former master.

Teaching for Jesuits was never an end in itself. They entered the field of Catholic action when Catholic education was in a parlous state. Because they saw education as a powerful means for restoring the Catholic faith in Europe, the Jesuits founded and developed their colleges wholeheartedly. Practical men make excellent copyists. Ignatius borrowed two-thirds of his Spiritual Exercises from other sources: only the verve and sense of purpose was his own. The Jesuit *Ratio Studiorum* was an amalgam of pedagogic methods that the early Jesuits found to work. Though scholastically trained, when it came to the rising generation they deliberately chose a humanist approach. Drama, sundials, fireworks, geography, the pagan classics were used, without any disguise, to fashion Christian men.

One cannot hope to understand the Jesuits, their Victorian schools, their mounting problems at the turn of the twentieth century unless their basic attitude to education
[303] is recognized. It would be unfair to suggest the Society never appreciated art or language as good in themselves: in classics in particular Jesuits became too much absorbed and much too precious, but the Order viewed all

education as a means to an end. By the end of the seventeenth century it has been estimated that the Jesuits in
Europe conducted more than 500 colleges. In all of these
the Fathers gave their services free. A great many Jesuits
were happy to spend their whole lives in the classroom in
order that the ideals that they themselves had learned, not
in the universities but in the Spiritual Exercises, should
survive.

Walloon Jesuits, with a large school next door to St
Omers, questioned the need for it. The question was
answered by a most distinguished member of their own
Province, Fr Giles Schondonck. Fr Giles grasped that the
survival of English Catholic culture and traditions turned
on the education of the Catholic boys. By his high standards he gave to the English exiles a sense of pride. It was
a boarding school while Jesuits favoured day schools and
it restricted its intake to English children; unconsciously
relaxed in the 18th century, the College retained its
national characteristics to the end. Though often called a
seminary, no boy coming to St Omers was under an oblig-
ation to become a priest.   [304]

In 1880, the English Jesuits, now happily back in their
native country, circulated a hostile account of Jesuit
educational methods published in the *Pall Mall Gazette*.
The article was no doubt read with care by distinguished
Jesuit converts, among them Gerard Manley Hopkins,
Christie, Newman's companion at Littlemore, Hathaway,
former Dean of Worcester College Oxford, and Walford,
one time housemaster at Eton. The writer accused Jesuits
of resisting independence of spirit in their boys and
dismissing those they could not curb, of too much supervision, encouraging tale telling, reducing all their boys to
a standard type. He praises them however for the trouble
taken with less intelligent pupils and their talent for devel-
oping a boy's aptitudes.

Those who have read the essay of Charles Lamb on his
Charterhouse days will judge Jesuits more tolerantly.
Even Arnold of Rugby might have viewed St Omers with

delight. In the first place the College was comprehensive,
[305] with no entrance examination to exclude the dull. The
Jesuits were still medieval enough to resent any form of
education that viewed a career as a goal. They accepted
any boy at any age and gave their full attention to the task
of fashioning him into a socially-balanced and well-read
Christian. They failed in many cases as with David
Maurice who finished by drawing a government pension
along with Dr Serjeant and Titus Oates.

Charles Wharton, twice married and a very distinguished parson, is perhaps the most eloquent witness for
the defence. The Jesuits he attests endeavoured to lay the
foundations of a strict morality, nay Christian piety, in the
minds of youth in their care. He felt pleasure in the indul-
gent recollections that, at an early period of his life many
great principles of religion had been planted in his mind
which had continued to be his guides and support. These
grateful feelings for his early instructors he said he would
ever cherish.

The boys at St Omers moved from the school of rudi-
ments, grammar, syntax, poetry, rhetoric before
transferring to Liège for a course in philosophy. The
Jesuits could not escape the medieval system: drama,
music, languages, grammar and poetry had ideally to be
[306] topped by philosophy. For the English Jesuits of this
period, that young man was educated who had completed
his humanities. They were perfected at St Omers, after
which it was hoped they would pass to Liège for a course
in philosophy. The lay students at Liège lived apart from
the Jesuit community with their own common room and
refectory. In Victorian days Stonyhurst similarly accom-
modated lay philosophers.

The master of each school at St Omers had a number of
young Jesuits to assist him. He himself was more than a
housemaster, in that he lived with and for the boys. In
theory at least he travelled with them through grammar to
rhetoric. He selected their texts, set their examinations,
organized their recreations, planned their dramatics and

composed their class plays. Each school kept its patronal feast, its Academy day, its Concertatio before the assem- [307] bled Fathers during dinner. The pupils were divided into Romans and Carthaginians and each boy had his opponent with whom he competed. The master of each school studied the character of each boy, giving special attention to such faults as shyness and lack of confidence.

Men as distinguished as Archbishop Goodier, Peter Gallwey and Herbert Thurston were first trained as masters of a school. On his journey to England Campion still had half his heart and mind on his boys at Prague. Many Jesuits were learned but only in the schoolroom sense. In the days when so many were illiterate, schoolmasters passed as learned. A great many Jesuit authors wrote with a neat and punctilious style, and all were grounded in the classics. They were in demand when they left the classroom for they now went as chaplains to the boys they had once taught. St Omers itself became a repository of treasures through the affection of alumni. With the Universities barred to Catholics, it was for many the dominant interest in a restricted life. Its faults were certainly covered by its virtues: in the cause of Catholic recusancy for which it alone was founded, its influence was extraordinary.

After the fall of the Stuarts, St Omers became the centre of a shrinking Jesuit world. The seminaries overseas were [308] now an embarrassment. Neither Persons nor Allen had ever imagined that they would be trying to function a century after his death. The fall of the Stuarts put an end to the divine right of kings, to all hope of toleration and a great deal of Counter-Reformation thought. Vocations to the priesthood dropped in quality and number. The whole system started to collapse. In 1763 two of the very few candidates at Valladolid decided to become Jesuits and the General, Lorenzo Ricci accepted the Vicars Apostolics' appeal. The English College in Rome was equally dejected. [309] The only sign of life came when in 1766 Prince Charles Edward was welcomed at the English, Irish and Scots

Colleges, attending Mass at the first. The rectors of these Colleges were instantly removed from office and sent out of Rome by Clement XIII. Moves were made to take the English College from the Jesuits. They were under fire world wide, especially in Rome, and this bred a form of touchiness.

Bishop Challenor complained that the Jesuits now provided few vocations to the secular clergy. The pressure on St Omers as one of the few flourishing centres in a dying system was unfair. Fr Richard Plowden put the case bluntly in 1725. He had but five boys in rhetoric and [310] twelve in poetry. The new property laws were impoverishing English Catholics; parents had no wish to send sons to Spain; the boys themselves had no desire to become priests.

In the last sixty years of St Omers the English College remained lively. It survived fires in 1684 and 1725, the latter more serious, and a fine new building was erected by 1727. Though the Society was now bitterly attacked, the system went on smoothly. In the main the standard of religious observance was high, a fact borne out in the years after the Order was abolished when men of the type of Charles Plowden and John Carroll could look back tearfully to the strict religious discipline of the good old days.

In every part of Flanders the young Jesuits worked for [311] the English and Irish soldiers in the Continental wars. The hero of this crusade, Fr John Clarke, was a native of Kilkenny; he seems to have spent his whole priestly life in Belgium; his missions to the soldiers started in 1696 and ended when he died in 1723.

The Jesuit image was adjusted to fit the facts. After the first exciting years and the long period in hiding, the English Jesuit turned into a schoolmaster and little more. The average Jesuit spent two years in the noviceship, some seven years at his scholastic studies, a year of final probation and nearly twenty years in the classroom. It was, as we have seen, some twenty-three years before Nicholas Blundell came home to see his family. When he returned

he met a world completely strange. After the Glorious
Revolution, severity to Catholics was greater than realized
and such repression would continue for seventy years.
There were no executions now though a few old Jesuits
lingered long in prison. But if savagery was passing, so
was hope. There were fewer crypto-Catholics or hidden
sympathizers. Catholics were excluded from Parliament,
the army, the universities. Advancement meant apostasy
throughout the eighteenth century and it was frequent
and understandable. The fourth Lord Baltimore publicly
abjured to recover his Maryland possessions. Molyneuxs [312]
and Talbots fell away, and a surprising number of priests.
At least two Jesuits were among them: Fr Jenison in 1772,
who returned to the Church twelve years later; Fr Charles
Wharton, a cousin of John Carroll was a professor at Liège
when the Society was suppressed. He worked in Worcester in the War of American Independence, and once back
in Maryland became an Episcopalian. In 1785 he was
rector of Immanuel Church, Newcastle, Delaware but his
profound spiritual crisis affected his health. He lived a
quiet, retired life, and though elected President of Colum-
bia University in 1801 ill health lead to early retirement.
Though John Carroll had had to reply to his *Letter* saying
why he became a Protestant, the two were on good terms
and Wharton always defended the Society.

The practice of the Catholic faith in England required
courage and stamina. Apart from restrictive laws on prop- [313]
erty and social status, informers could collect a reward for
denouncing a priest. On two occasions the English Provincial had to postpone his visitations of England and in 1744
his house in London was searched. Anti-papist riots were
organized whenever a secret Catholic chapel was disclosed. In 1746 the first Catholic chapel in Liverpool was [314]
destroyed, while in the Gordon riots of 1780 a rumour
went round that 20,000 Jesuits were ready to blow up the
banks of the Thames and drown all Londoners.

Yet the eighteenth-century Jesuits, despite hardships,
seem as hopeful and far more calm and cheerful than in

earlier days. The tempo of Catholic life was slower and the
false hopes raised by the Stuarts were gone forever. The
Church survived in rural areas where friendships come
more easily; in certain districts there was a marked
ecumenical charity. The Church survived through the
good services of the faithful landed gentry, many of them
old St Omers boys – the Petres, Blundells, Tempests,
Gerards, Scarisbricks, Welds and Arundels.

[315]   The *Province note and address book* lists Jesuits hideouts.
They served over 100 missions, a great many Jesuits were
chaplains to Catholic families but a surprising number
shifted for themselves. Facilities for community life were
easier in the north west and north east. The Provincial
made his regular visitations, often yearly. Jesuits could
come to Durham, where Catholics were still numerous, to
meet the Provincial. Many of these missionaries were men
of outstanding character. The pocket book of Fr Henry
Scarisbrick, with entries of Mass intentions, almsgiving,
letters overseas, money payments, provide a picture of
[316] Lancashire life. Fr Robert Aldred, chaplain at Crosby, was
delightful and witty, arguing with Pastor Waring, helping
innumerable simple Catholics in the art of dying, and
teaching the squire how to balance an egg on a mirror's
edge. The Squire of Crosby's brother, Fr Joseph Blundell,
was an amateur art collector, with an attraction for inven-
tories. He drew up a list of furnishings at Selby, belonging
in the Jesuit jargon of the period, to 'Mrs York'.

Meanwhile from the north east Fr Layton sends a vivid
letter describing the heroic efforts of Fr Janion for the
dying. Ill-mounted, he would take on rivers in time of
[317] flood when fords were thought by others to be impassable.
In his ministry Fr Newton in Suffolk is discouraged in
having to ride forty or fifty miles east, west and north to
be met with ignorance, stupidity and neglect of religion,
but a letter from Charles Plowden cheers him up. Fr
Newton's excursions, frustrating though they were,
seem trivial beside the vast expeditions undergone by
English Jesuits in eighteenth-century Maryland. Fr Joseph

Greaton, whose home in England had been near to the headlands that skirt the Bristol Channel, took in New York, New Jersey and Pennsylvania in an active life of eighteen years. Later from the same base, a German Jesuit, changing his name to Farmer, would evangelize Delaware and New Jersey. Fr Robert Molyneux, stout and not too [318] good on journeys, minded the parish and kept the books. These two Jesuits were together on the sanctuary when on March 1st 1781 a solemn Te Deum was chanted in thanksgiving for French aid in the War of American Independence.

One last journey takes us from Philadelphia to Shropshire where a remarkable English Jesuit resided for some time as chaplain to the Plowden family. Thomas Falkner, a Protestant surgeon, went as ship's doctor on the *Asiento* to Brazil. Converted by the kindness of the Portuguese Jesuits he entered the Society and served thirty-eight years in Paraguay. A learned man, who had written a book about this distant mission, he was expelled to England when the Society's problems there were at their height. Of vast experience and many stories, he greatly interested Frs Oliver and John Thorpe. An old memory survives that he boiled his meat in his hat, and it being saturated by fat, the dog ate it.

The mention of Paraguay brings the tragedy of the Jesuits a step nearer. In 1752, the Jesuit General Lorenzo Ricci appealed to all Provinces for financial assistance to aid the missionaries now expelled from Portuguese territory by Pombal. News travelled slowly and English Jesuits [319] knew next to nothing of the sufferings of their Spanish and Portuguese brethren until victims like Falkner arrived. Another English Jesuit from Brazil, Fr Francis Atkins, was brought back to Lisbon in 1759 to rot in a Portuguese prison for nearly eighteen years. He died three months after his release.

The existence of the Society was now threatened in all the Bourbon countries. That the College at St Omers, so famous as a foreign school, might have escaped seemed at

one time possible. The Jesuits still had many friends. They
also had powerful enemies determined to destroy them at
any cost. The sordid intrigues which lead to the abandon-
ment of the College hardly concern us here. One of the
clearest of the accounts of negotiations was written by Fr
Reeve. Reeve confirms the opinion of a document now in
the Westminster archives, that the *Parlement* of Paris was
induced chiefly by Lady Webb's good offices to exempt
the English College from ruin. The favour did not take
place on account of information brought against them
[320] by some respectable clergy of their own race. Bishops
Challenor and Hornyold felt shame and embarrassment
knowing well that this was an indirect blow at the Pope.

Challenor's position was unenviable; he had to consider
the needs of his poverty-stricken English church. Could he
honestly have refused the College offered him by the
French authorities? Rome was asked to decide and the
[320] answer was that the offer be accepted, with priests from
Douai being asked to take it over. By the time the envoys
[321] from Douai had arrived the Jesuits had departed with
boys, furniture and equipment to reopen their college in
Bruges. Fr Brown, aged ninety-two, and Fr Hawder at
seventy-seven stayed, with Br Stephens as infirmarian.

Fr Thomas Lawson of Brough Hall, Yorkshire, their
determined agent in Paris, fought every point doggedly,
and discovered that there was a plan afoot to prevent the
boys being moved. They were less happy with their
Provincial Fr Henry Corbie, in bed with fever; it was said
he was better versed in spiritual than in temporal affairs.
The rector of St Omers, Fr Francis Scarisbrick at this
[322] critical time, was equally ineffective.

The man for the crisis was Fr John Darrel, the Procurator. By sheer chance, one of the Fathers had kept up a
casual correspondence with a relative now in the magistry
of Bruges. Through this contact a suitable building was
purchased, while Fr George Mannock played a part in
gaining permission for it from Vienna, with full protection
for it. Darrel also opened negotiations for the house at

Bruges, arranged for the departure of the boys, and the storing of treasures and food for the journey. Everything had to be done in secret. The townsfolk would resent the departure of the famous College. The *Parlement* only wanted the Jesuits out. The boys stuffed their pockets with a few essentials and set off, as if on a school jaunt, and a barge took them to Watten where food was provided, the [323] first party reaching Bruges exhausted on 11th August. Other boys arrived in due course. The students were there before the townsmen of St Omers knew a single person had left the college. The parents of the children approved all that had been done. In Bruges the Jesuits acquired two buildings and opened a junior and senior school. The townsfolk were courteous; the English nuns and the Austin friars did much to help the furnishing. The two colleges would survive ten years with over a hundred students and almost as many on the waiting list.

10

The suppression of the Society

The Brief of Suppression was not promulgated until 16th August 1773 so that the great Church of the Jesu could for the last time wear its trappings to honour St Ignatius on his feast. On 31st July the Jesuit General Fr Lorenzo Ricci still saw grounds for hope. He found it hard to believe that the Vicar of Christ would burden his conscience with so blatant an injustice as the destruction of the Society. The Emperor Joseph of Austria put it more clearly. He judged it impossible that any pope would ever consent to fire upon his best and most useful troops.

[326] The Pope supported his case with other historical examples of suppression going back to the Knights Templars in 1321 but this comparison is halting for in the magnitude of its destruction the suppression of the Society is unique. In 1750, the year before the Portuguese attack, the Society had numbered 22,589 members, in forty-two Provinces, 669 colleges, 61 noviciates, 335 residences and 273 mission stations. Whatever the charges against them, the Jesuits could look back with pride to this massive achievement and they certainly did. That there had been faults in the Jesuit machine no Jesuit would deny. The Order may have grown too great, too monopolistic and in an unexpected way, too conservative. A heterogenous army of rivals united against the Order: the French encyclopedists, bitter against religion, the Jansenists, the Regalists, the colonial

exploiters and a clique of curial money grubbers out for immediate gain.

The Society was not overthrown without a long and bitter struggle, for it still enjoyed the loyal support of many friends. When the act was done and the Jesuit voice was silent a great many powerful advocates defended its name. Thus Christopher Beaumont, Archbishop of Paris, wrote personally to the Pope, that the brief which destroyed the Society is nothing else than an isolated, private and pernicious judgement which does no honour to the Tiara and is prejudicial to the glory of the Church and to the growth and conservation of the orthodox faith. [327] The encyclopedist Duclos did not hesitate to declare that the Provinces of France regret the loss of the Jesuits and they would if they were to reappear among them, be received with acclamation. It was fear of such support that compelled the Roman Curia to act so secretly. On the 16th August, the General was arrested, observing that whatever the Pope decided did not need his concurrence. He was moved to the Castel Sant' Angelo to die two years later, never having been brought to trial. The Jesuits in Rome were forced to sign an act of submission. They could apply to a bishop as secular priests. On the part of ex-Jesuits there was no resistance of any kind. [328]

Fr John Carroll of Maryland, aged thirty-six, came to Rome just before the suppression. He tells of the intrigues, the propaganda, the scurrilous attacks made on the Society. We know that he dared not disclose his identity [329] and hesitated to call on his brethren. He returned to Bruges, bitter and indignant at Roman decadence. He met Charles Plowden and the English Jesuit agent John Thorpe, a pious Yorkshireman of virulent wit. Thorpe in his endless correspondence with Plowden, John Carroll, Lord Arundel and others, covered the art, politics, gossip and scandals of eighteenth-century Rome. Up to his death in 1792, he continued his work for his former brethren. Much loved, and an art collector of distinction, he never forgot the injustice to the Society.

The suppression ended the Province but the dissolution affected different houses differently. The greatest disasters fell on Bruges. Frs Ashton and Angier, rectors of the Colleges, asked permission to continue them as secular [330] priests. The Bishop assured them all would be well. He was at best a dupe. The Austrian government at Brussels, bitterly anti-Jesuit, had other plans. They wanted the English school to remain for reasons of trade, prestige and money, after which the Jesuits would be out. They had been raising funds for their new building. The authorities hoped to find them in the house. On 20th September, the commissioners deposed the rectors and searched the premises. Workmen probed every wall, floor, ceiling, beam, desk and table, before retiring in vexation and disappointment, leaving a scene of desolation.

On 14th October, soldiers surrounded the Colleges and the ex-Jesuits were lead away. The wretched men were not [331] even allowed to go to their rooms. Frs Angier, Plowden and Carroll were driven to the College of the Flemish Fathers and kept in strict durance. English Dominicans were brought in their place: they had not much choice. When the Jesuits had been taken away, the school could not be controlled. Order was at an end. The boys flew to the gates and were held back by bayonets. They grew desperate. Some forced through windows and over walls, others broke everything. The greater number of those who escaped were taken in by local families. Several of the students were carried off under arms. In the end, Frs Angier and Richard Morgan were marched back to [332] persuade the boys to go to bed.

The heroine throughout was the Augustinian Prioress, sister to the English Provincial and one of the last direct descendants of St Thomas More. Dame Margaret and her chaplain bailed out the boys, wrote to parents and salvaged what they could of the building, including the body of the Roman martyr St Gordian. Promised to Lancashire in 1667, it arrived at Stonyhurst with swinging [333] thuribles in 1862. The majority of the ex-Jesuits were released after a week, with orders to quit the Netherlands for good. Only Frs Ashton, Angiers and Charles Plowden were detained in the hope they would surrender the mythical treasure and the boys' fees. They were under arrest for eight months, supplied with all necessities and a mail service by Dame Margaret and other conspirators until, through the good services of Lord Arundel of Wardour, they were released.

At Liège the treatment of the Jesuits was very different; the Brief of Suppression took them by surprise. Certain signs of upset had troubled the men there, one being the number of exiled French Jesuits living with the community, another a more recent letter from Fr Ricci on 11th April begging prayers for the Society. The students no [334] doubt said some prayers for the intention but their minds were on their holiday at Chevremont. On Friday 3rd September they set out for Liège. On their way they passed some of their professors from whom they heard that the Society had been suppressed; the students hurried home and made for the chapel in their distress. When on the Saturday morning the Brief of Dissolution arrived they could not believe that a document so full of lies had been issued by the Vicar of Christ.

The publication of the Brief had been fixed for 9th September. On the fatal day three Monsignori inspected the house, sealed the archives and library, asked certain questions of each member of the community and concluded with an address to the whole. The ex-Jesuits were reminded [335] they were no longer religious, the students were free to return to the lay state, the priests could present themselves to a bishop. The deposed rector moved to a nearby convent to which he was appointed chaplain, and a diocesan ppriest was installed in his place. The senior Fathers began slowly to drift away. Sorrow was turned to joy when Fr Charles Neale arrived with three companions from Ghent. The theological course started in October. The survival of the College at Liège was totally unexpected. The Prince Bishop of the city was kindly disposed to the

[336]   English ex-Jesuits, largely from self-interest. An English College at Liège was of commercial interest to his subjects and a feather for the Diocese. He had acquired a fine building, a staff of unpaid masters and the prospect of boys' fees. He was his own master, unlike the Bishop of Bruges. The Jesuits were duly grateful for the survival of the College but it was not a sign of affection for the Society.

On 27th October the first party of boys from Bruges arrived. Others followed, and on 15th December the Prince Bishop proclaimed the opening of the Liège Academy and made Fr John Howard, the former Jesuit rector, the first President. It was a hotchpotch but its numbers, which were 27 in 1773, were 144 by 1776. The Prince Bishop applied to Rome seeking pardon in case he had offended against the Brief, but, in reply, the new Pope blessed his admirable act, and granted the status of Pontifical College to the Liège Academy. While Rome smiled on Liège, Charles Plowden, now at Lulworth, was for ever rumbling and grumbling at the damage done to the

[337]   terraced gardens to make room for more boys.

In Maryland we find an atmosphere of shame and humiliation. As there were no bishops there, and the majority of the priests were Jesuits, the wretched Fathers

[338]   had to suppress themselves. Twenty-one signed their acceptances. This was the end of the English mission to America. The Maryland ex-Jesuits, after many bitter struggles, would rise again. The *Destructive Brief* as it was called, was brought to England by Monsignor Stonor. Challoner had misgivings about sending it through the Protestant post, and invited the twenty-six London Jesuits, headed by Fr Thomas More, the last English Provincial, to call on him to complete the humiliating act; they availed themselves of this choice. Challoner showed great kindness and sympathy to the victims.

Thomas More was the last direct male descendant of the Lord Chancellor. Charles Plowden, normally critical, greatly admired this last Provincial, four years in office during a sad and difficult time. More set out the financial position of the defunct Province in a personal interview. He pointed out that he had his obligations to those who had given up all their property to the Society and that which was necessary for the aged and infirm. Challoner agreed to his arrangements, and More promised that all monies would be directed to the English mission after such obligations had been met.

The Vicars Apostolic behaved with great sympathy. [339] Challenor not only wrote to Rome in favour of Liège, but renewed the faculties for the London Jesuits and permitted them to govern themselves, Thomas More being made his Vicar for the purpose. John Gage, sending Bishop Hornyhold his submission, tells of his love for the Society, to which he said he owed all the little learning and virtue he had. Hornyhold renews his faculties, and begs him to use his temporalities as before. The misery expressed in Gage's letter is repeated by many other ex-Jesuits, all of whom suffered a profound shock. John Carroll, in a series of letters to Charles Plowden, could more freely disclose [340] his mind. I can assure you, he wrote in 1782, that one of his strongest inducements to leave Europe was to be removed out of sight and hearing of those scenes of iniquity, duplicity and depredation of which I had seen and heard so much. Carroll does not believe rumours that the Society would be restored because this would be opposed by the united voice and efforts of those plunderers who have enriched themselves with the lands of the Society, the furniture and the colleges, the plate and treasure of the churches and sacrasties.

For two dark years, both in England and Maryland, little or nothing could be done. The older ex-Jesuits were too dejected to move. Joseph Reeve recalls of this period, that the unassuming Mr More declined taking a lead in the common cause. Finally a meeting was called on 26th April, with Joseph Reeve, a bundle of energy, acting as secretary, and also representing the old Devonshire district while William Strickland spoke for Durham, Jenner for Suffolk and all the other colleges sent a representative. Thomas

More was not allowed to resign. Indeed he and the former
[341] procurator, Thomas Talbot were to administer a central
office and to be paid £100 a year, a humiliating but necessary item. The loss of the vow of poverty led the Fathers to
fear the day when self-interest would corrupt the spirit of
self-sacrifice. At this meeting they had to consider care of
the old ex-Jesuits working in poorer districts. In the end,
not entirely with the spirit one might have expected,
London, Derby, Suffolk, Hampshire and Lincoln agreed to
subsidize their colleagues in Durham, Yorkshire, Worcester and Devonshire. One ray of hope lightened a gloomy
congress. Liège reported how the College had survived.

A second more cheerful meting was held at the Queen's
[342] Head tavern in Holborn in July 1784. The most significant
change was the making of William Strickland the representative for Liège, John Howard having died in the
previous year. The weary Thomas More refused another
term at central office; Strickland offered his services and
was accepted. With Strickland's arrival the affairs of the
ex-Jesuits altered rapidly. Be it noted that the second
anniversary of Campion's *Brag* could not be honoured.
The English Province was no more. The majority of ex-
Jesuits returned to their districts in England as diocesan
priests. Some used their pensions to send boys to Liège.

Others, later criticized by Plowden and Glover had
disposed of their portion of the Jesuit property to their
districts or build churches. The suppression came when
the first signs of religious tolerance were showing in
England. Ex-Jesuits set about building churches in
[343] Preston, Liverpool, Worcester and Hereford. The famous
Daddy Dunn, for a time the bane of Charles Plowden's
life, became a celebrity in Preston with his House of
Recovery, the fine Church of St Wilfrids, Catholic schools
and gasworks.

The majority of ex-Jesuits were not spared to see the
restoration of the Society. John Thorpe died in Rome,
leaving all his possessions to his dear Academy at Liège.
Fr John Butler, tenth Lord Cahir, rejected the Bishopric of

Limerick. He died at Hereford after serving the mission
1760–86. Pere Grou never learned English; he lived at
Lulworth, in a very small room, dividing his time between
writing and prayer. Two hundred years later his reputation as a mystic has not declined. His books have a depth
not surpassed in any age.   [344]

In the thirty years before the Restoration one hundred
and twenty-seven of the members of the Province died
where they had worked for years. At least seven descendants of St Thomas More had been Jesuits. For seventy
years (1773–1843) the story of the Province is the story of
the Academy in Liège, continued at Stonyhurst. This may
seem dull to those who prefer their history in large sensational slices, but happily there are others with a deep
appreciation of the day-to-day efforts of simple and
devoted men.   [345]

It might be claimed that William Strickland,
Marmaduke Stone and Charles Plowden measure up to
the greatest in the centuries between Campion and
Martindale. William Strickland comes first, born in
Sizergh, the family estate near Kendal in 1731, and to
which he was heir. He relinquished his heritage to his
younger brother to enter the Society at Watten in 1748. We
know he pronounced his final vows in 1766. He was then
a Jesuit for seven years before the Suppression. For a while
a professor at Liège, he returned to England to work on
the the mission in Durham for perhaps twelve years.
Strickland was fifty-three when he found himself President of Liège.

A man of intelligence and vigour he grasped the situation, recognized that the men senior to himself were now
too dejected and a lead must be given by someone, so why
not him? How else to explain his sudden offer to administer the central office when he was also President? He was
a diocesan priest. The Academy had no funds to support
it. In the end the Fathers at Holborn agreed to help in the
financing; a coalition and connexion of direction and
dependence was formed between the mission and the

[346]   Academy. When Strickland took in hand the administration of Liège not all Jesuits were optimistic about the future. The Prince Bishop's financial commitments were nil. The masters would have to be paid, they were jaded, some wanted extra pay for extra work. Strickland in the five years he held the double office brought order out of chaos, bringing the number of boys up to a steady hundred, and establishing bursaries. John Carroll provided a number of German students to be trained for
[347]   the priesthood for an expanding American Church.

Revival of morale was aided by a number of Jesuits, certainly by Thomas and Joseph Reeve. Liège was school and seminary in one. Strickland and his advisers made up their minds that the young seminarians be trained in the traditions that they had known in their Jesuit days: a daily hour of meditation, spiritual reading, and silence outside the time of official recreation. Early rising was recommended, four o'clock was to be tried, though leave could be got for five. Other documents concerned the formation of a congregation to make contact with former Jesuits now
[348]   working in England as secular priests.

During all this time Charles Plowden was acting as chaplain to Thomas Weld. As a secular priest, he was a man of social and literary distinction, still seeking to observe his Jesuit vows. He kept up a steady correspondence with Thorpe in Rome and Carroll in Maryland. During the War of American Independence they had differences. Carroll complained of the maraudings of English cruisers; Plowden was indignant that the colonists had been accepting aid from faithless leaders and their allies i.e. the French. Another long exchange turned on the hapless Charles Wharton, so soon to apostatize. Carroll also warned his friends that he would be made Superior of the mission: Thorpe informed him he was the obvious choice of a bishop for America. Plowden received the plans for the proposed College at Georgetown: he was invited to take over the direction of studies or find a substitute.

[349]   Plowden undertook a bold literary venture at this time;

the story of the Jesuits in White Russia who had survived. That they did so is due directly to the partition of Poland in 1771, which placed six or seven Polish Jesuit houses inside the Empire of Catherine the Great. The Empress was determined not to let them go. They were administering the only schools in the impoverished region. The enemies of the Jesuits snarled, the Polish Jesuits were hesitant and frightened. Clement XIV appears powerless and pathetic when dealing with a determined woman who knew her own mind. Plowden typically admires her vigour. He quotes her note to the Provincial telling him that you and all other Jesuits should obey the Pope in what concerns the Dogmas of religion: in all other respects your duty is to obey your sovereign. Since you are scrupulous, I shall concert measures with the Pope's nuncio.

So the Brief was never promulgated and both Clement and his successor had no option but to be resigned. By 1799 the Russian Jesuits had permission to open a noviceship because its ageing membership meant they would be unable to staff their schools. What was to stop novices [350] going to Russia from other parts of the world? Poles, Italians and Germans gladly did. At the Liège Academy, the announcement of the resurrection was viewed with delight. Plowden completed his manuscript, and in England, Flanders and Maryland it had an abiding effect. Thus in 1788, thirteen ex-Jesuits from Maryland drew up a petition for a link with the Jesuits in Russia. No more came [351] of it until the turn of the century.

John Carroll was nominated as first Bishop of Baltimore. He had many misgivings. When Quebec, Dublin and Rome were proposed as suitable places for his consecration, he extricated himself with considerable tact. He chose the beautiful chapel at Lulworth recently completed because he said it would enable him to see some of those friends whom he would ever honour and love. On Sunday 15th August 1790 Charles Plowden preached at his consecration Mass.

The ex-Jesuits were in better shape in 1790. The Russian

Jesuit Province was now fully confirmed, the Academy at Liège was more firmly established while a number of ex-Jesuits in England were now accepting a more than nominal authority of the President. It was now that Strickland resigned to manage the central office, a post he held for thirty-five years. From a variety of addresses, Edgware Road, Bayswater, Upper Berkeley Street and Poland Street, he gave his mind to the protection of Jesuit funds. Strickland had his eye on the English Province of the future, his one concern and conviction for the moment being the restoration of the Society. For this reason he fought a running battle with any bishop, any ex-Jesuits, or the Congregation of Propaganda, who tried to lay their hands on Jesuit property. It was not very considerable but what was left should be devoted to the cause for which it had been received.

The two purposes of Jesuit funds, quoting the rule of St Ignatius, were the salvation and perfection of the members of the Order and the salvation and perfection of their [352] neighbour. His disputes were impersonal and impartial. Ex-Jesuits who had at the time of the suppression, personal experience of clerical corruption, distrusted the Congregation of Propaganda and its minions. Too much had been stolen, too many had feathered their nests through the suppression, for men of the calibre of Carroll, Plowden or Strickland to feel any lasting confidence. These three and many more had sacrificed wealth and social position to become religious, and were not simple enough to be fobbed off while some dubious cleric, sheltered by his Roman collar, made away with the church plate. The Church in this period had sowed distrust. In the case of Strickland this should be noted, his anger fell as [353] savagely on ex-Jesuits as on others. Strickland's point was that they were to consider the Society as a common parent and on the demise of that parent the property could descend nowhere with so great propriety as on the children of that parent. Strickland was prepared to invoke a possible breach of praemunire should the fate of Jesuit properties be decided by the Congregation of Propaganda in Rome.

We may part with William Strickland here. In middle age he had left the Durham mission in a time of crisis, undertook the Presidency at Liège and then took over the central office in London with sensational success. He never went to Russia but he played a crucial part in the final union of the Gentlemen of Liège and Stonyhurst with the rump there. He it was who made the first contacts, drew up a list of names of Jesuits who would welcome affiliation and recommended Fr Marmaduke Stone as first Provincial. In the final stages he handed over the work to others, fearing to form a third party between Stone and the Plowdens or become an eminence grise. We now know that Strickland would have been Provincial himself had not the Russian Superior thought him too old and weak, a verdict not based on the hidden toughness of this remarkable man. Strickland renewed his vows as a Jesuit in 1803 and survived at the central office for another sixteen years. He died in 1819 and was buried in St Pancras churchyard, an eminent and patriarchal gentleman. [354]

Fr Marmaduke Stone, both as President of Liège and later as first Provincial, well illustrates the wisdom of Strickland. With one eye on the Plowdens, Charles and Robert, sons of thunder, Strickland once gave his reasons for promoting Stone. He was a man loved by all who knew him. If humility, mildness and piety can deserve esteem, he must be esteemed. A man of more active disposition as well as decision might easily have been found, and would have advanced the object by bolder and more vigorous measures, but in our circumstances I do not think this necessary.

Mr Stone was without doubt the oddest Provincial that the English Jesuits ever knew. In face and figure corpulent and cherubic, he could do nothing to invest his features with the emaciation which ordinarily attends the habits of mortification and self-denial he practised. An alumnus wrote on his appointment that I think his reverence is too [355] much absorbed in heavenly things to be fit for this mission. Mr Stone was to govern the English Jesuits for twenty-seven years – an all-time record since the Province was first established under Richard Blount.

Stone was born in 1748, early enough to have known St Omers, and died in 1834, late enough to see the English Province fully restored. As a small boy he went to Watten, next to St Omers, and was probably one of those who made the trek to Bruges. Dates alone can guide us, because he rarely did anything outstanding enough to earn a mention in any manuscript. He finished his school career at Bruges and made his noviceship at Ghent. Of his studies at Ghent we know little more than the beadle tells us in his logbook: he was an expert in catching moles. At the time of the suppression, Stone was a student at Liège. He was ordained there in 1775, and became master of the school of elements, the bottom class, for fourteen years when he was suddenly elected President in Strickland's [356] place.

The Bastille had just fallen and a group of patriots seized the Citadel in Liège, just above the College. In 1791 the Austrians occupied the city and were driven out by the French in November 1792. Soldiers were billeted in the College and the bursar, Fr Charles Wright, son of a London banker, did them well. The French were again expelled. In 1793 Louis XVI was executed and Liège was no longer safe for Englishmen. The offer that, should the Academy move to England, it could find asylum in Weld's derelict mansion at Stonyhurst, was made about this time. The departure turned into a scramble and on 14th June 1794 the Jesuits left. They were lucky in their chronicler, Fr Laurenson, in Charles Wright their Procurator, and the timely arrival of John O'Shea, an alumnus and an officer in the Austrian army who prevented his men commandeering their only horse. The flight was at once hilarious and tragic, in that they lost many books and instruments, while the hurriedly buried coffin of Peter Wright the martyr was [357] never to be found again. Each boy carried what he could.

Tradition has it that the President, Fr Stone, filled his pockets with pepper pots.

They sailed down the Meuse in leaking barges. At Rotterdam a ship was procured for them by a former brother who, after the suppression, had become a merchant and prospered as such. So the English Jesuits left Flanders after two centuries. They stopped at Harwich, and here some of the party left them to visit their families. The remainder went on by boat to Hull, then on to Selby by barge, where the citizens took them for Frenchmen and shouted that the rascals deserved all they got for killing their king. The next leg of their journey carried them by canal through Leeds to Skipton. Here Frs Semes and Ellerker hired a carriage. The rest covered the last twenty-five miles on foot. Fr Ellerker was an invalid and would last but eight months longer.

The first days at Stonyhurst were of overcrowding and discomfort. The mansion was not a large one, and had [358] been uninhabited for years. The extraordinary vitality of Fr Charles Wright soon put the school in shape. Charles Plowden was doubtful about Wright' s taste, but his aims were practical He threw up a building condemned as hideous, but still serviceable after one hundred and fifty years. Within two months the St Omers machine was in operation, the *Ascensio Scholarum* with forty pupils being held on 24th October. In all these initial excitements little is recorded of the President, Mr Stone. He went to Whalley with his community to take the oath of allegiance only to find that rumour had it they were French spies. It was highly laughable that Plowden should be called upon to prove he was no foreigner. [359]

More worrying and frustrating were the long misunderstandings with Dr William Gibson, Vicar Apostolic of the Northern District. He faced an unusual situation with a Pontifical Seminary, manned by ex-Jesuits and protected by a foreign bishop, thus unexpectedly established in his territory. Dr Gibson received the exiles kindly and was well-intentioned, inviting them to forget all past divisions between Douai and Liège, for ex-Jesuits were diocesan priests and a bishop enjoys the right of appointment of a seminary President. The Gentlemen of Liège were also well-intentioned and saw themselves as quasi religious, protected by a papal brief. They were also suspicious of Dr Gibson. While the college was sailing down the Meuse, Plowden writes to Lord Arundel telling of Gibson's unwillingness that any other house of education be attempted, save that near Durham. Thomas Glover recalls the amusement of the scholars when in an address Dr Gibson spoke of Stonyhurst as his college.

[360]

Such frictions were not the fault of either party, but derived from the ridiculous situation. Mr Stone acted with surprising speed; the papal brief was confirmed. Stonyhurst was to enjoy the privilege, not fully defined, of a pontifical college. It should be noted that the Gentlemen of Liège at the time probably saw no permanent home in Lancashire and intended to return to Liège when the war had been won. Marmaduke Stone had moved swiftly on this one occasion; normally his reactions were very slow. All the evidence suggests he was totally ill-equipped for government, yet no other Jesuit, Plowden included, could have survived so many critical situations to emerge untroubled and universally loved. He had an unending capacity for seeking advice though he rarely followed it; at least he listened and in so doing eased the frustrations of his complex community. For nearly four hundred years no Jesuit superior was ever asked to govern so odd a community. Stone normally did nothing, and his wisdom has echoed down the years.

[361]

Marmaduke Stone faced his second crisis with the arrival of the Paccanarists in 1800, who were seeking recruits in England. The Society of the Faith, its popular title deriving from its founder Paccanari, had adopted the rule of the suppressed Society and an identical apostolate. One omits with sorrow Tournely, the true founder, and Varin, a one-time French army officer and a dynamic influence on the post-revolution French Church. By the time the Society of the Faith came to England, Paccanari had successfully rallied support and the rapid extension of this new congregation flattered the despondent ex-Jesuits; it showed that many young men still valued the ideals of St Ignatius.

The mystery of the Paccanarists was how a new Ignatian order could spread throughout the Church, apparently with Roman approval, where the old-time ex-Jesuits had been disowned, and canonically disapproved. They opened a small retreat house, a girls' and a boys' school in London. Initial success was extraordinary. The ex-Jesuits alone were wary because they had made no secret of their intention to draw ex-Jesuits into their Institute. Paccanari was a former member of the papal guard, and the majority of his associates Frenchmen. The Paccanarists tasted a success in Catholic and Protestant London that no English ex-Jesuit would ever enjoy. Yet something was wrong. Their eyes were fixed on Stonyhurst but by the end of 1800 they had collected only one English ex-Jesuit, Charles Forrester, who had made a retreat with them and was confident that the new congregation met all the Jesuit requirements. He joined them though he eventually returned to his ex-Jesuit companions. [363]

[362]

An intense but passing flutter disturbed the ex-Jesuits at the first Paccanarist approach. The newcomers offered an easy way of escape. No hope of any restoration of the Society had been aired in 1800, and here were devoted men, Jesuit in all but name. Yet Forrester excepted, no English ex-Jesuit would accept such a substitute. Strickland is most suspicious, suspecting that a group of cardinals, fearing the revival of the Jesuits, is pushing Paccanari as a substitute. He was not alone in his suspicions; Nicholas Sewall, Carroll, Plowden and Simpson had theirs.

Two outstanding Paccanarists, De Broglie and Rozaven, arrived at Stonyhurst in early 1801. All accounts show that charity and affection were mutual. Yet there were weird overtones: for there were two young Frenchmen, claiming to carry papal approval of the banner of Ignatius. Fr

[364]   Sewall writes that we all soon saw it would be very impru-
dent to unite with them. They were very unwilling to form
a connection with the Jesuits in Russia and seemed to wish
we should all fall under the standard of Fr Paccanari. Tom
Reeve, the most sympathetic, wrote that our final unani-
mous answer was that we were ready to unite with them
when they became united with the Society in White
Russia. Marmaduke Stone never opened his mouth. One
final comment remains from the conference. Their edifying behaviour confirmed the ex-Jesuits that, though not of
our Society, they were of God.

Scarcely had the two Paccanarists left the College when
Mr Stone heard a rumour that Pope Pius VII had finally
confirmed the Russian Jesuits by brief. It was so, the brief
Catholicae Fidei was dated 7th March 1801. Fr Strickland
promptly wrote to Russia begging leave to affiliate. The
reply was disappointing because it seemed the Pope had
limited the Polish General's jurisdiction to Russia, but a
second reply on 12th October 1802 said permission had
been granted for Russian Jesuits to accept aspirants
outside Russia under certain strict conditions.

In March 1803, the newly elected General, Fr Gabriel
Gruber, wrote from Russia naming Marmaduke Stone as
[365]   Provincial on Fr Strickland's advice. Gruber, in his letter to
Stone points out that the Pope had already suffered much
after his initial brief in favour of the Russian Jesuits, and that
no further brief would be issued to confirm this verbal
consent. Stone's position was intolerable. Gibson sent him a
statement issued by the Congregation of Propaganda
telling the English bishops not to recognize those who
wished to be Jesuits in England nor admit their privileges.
When the friendly Archbishop of Dublin wrote to question
Stone's authority for reviving the Jesuits in England, he
replied very humbly, making it clear that this verbal
permission of the Pope affected only the internal forum; that
Jesuits were only so in private. In public they were secular
priests. Stone hinted that if Propaganda doubted the valid-
[366]   ity of the permission it had only to ask the Holy Father.

Stone, a hesitant man, acted with great firmness on this. The word of the Russian General was a command for him. Following his suggestion he renewed his simple vows as a Jesuit, first pronounced in 1769. Finally in the presence of Fr Strickland he took the four vows of the solemnly professed and thus completed his Jesuit training, so rudely interrupted for exactly thirty years. Jesuit tradition [367] was scrupulously followed when the other ex-Jesuits renewed their vows. William Strickland and eight other venerable men who had been professed simply renewed their vows again. After a short pause, fifteen relatively younger men renewed their simple vows and went forward to solemn profession in the normal way. In all thirty-three priests and two brothers renewed their vows and thirty-four declined.

Some felt they were too old; others did not want to be a [368] burden. Some, with the Plowdens, feared another disappointment, and would not rejoin until they had a confirming brief. Carroll and Neale were US bishops and felt they had to consider the American Church. Carroll himself was suspicious of this verbal restoration. Charles Wright and others were, after so long a gap, inextricably involved in financial matters. Wright eventually set off to [369] make his retreat and renew his vows in 1827 but died at Whalley en route. Paccanari refused to accept the verbal assent: his death was violent and mysterious. The Jesuits in Russia were very afraid of any mass reception of Paccanarists into the Society and required of these earnest men to come to Russia and the noviceship. Fr Rosaven, one of those who came to Stonyhurst, later as a Jesuit held high office in Rome.

The school made good progress; by 1829 there were 120 pupils, a number regarded remarkable in those pre-Catholic emancipation days. In 1808 Fr Sewall, as rector, greatly extended the old Shireburn buildings. In the list of donors there were many old Jesuit names: the Welds, Arundells, Petres, Constables and others, the alumni of St Omers, Bruges, Liège or Stonyhurst. When Fr Stone renewed his vows and became Provincial he only added to his immediate worries. After 1803 the Gentlemen of Stony-hurst were split into four parties, all united only in love of [370]   the good Mr Stone. Those who had renewed their vows wanted to live like Jesuits again; others, like Charles Wright the procurator, were not bound by religious obedience. Both mixed with a group of students training for the priesthood and a further group of mature priests. Plowden touches on the muddle in 1814. Introducing Jesuit customs when only four of the diners were Jesuits would lead to the complaint that an attempt was made to make others Jesuits against their will. By art or artlessness Fr Stone kept the crazy craft moving forward for fourteen years.

On 26th September Fr Charles Plowden started a novi-tiate for twelve men at a small house a mile from the College. For the sake of secrecy a preparatory school was opened at Hodder to disguise the activities of the novices. Secrecy became almost an obsession with the Society not [371]   yet publicly restored. Jesuits must not be seen and heard. Charles Plowden, as chaplain at Lulworth and Wardour had a considerable reputation in Catholic society, had travelled widely, was an excellent preacher, a man of letters and a vigorous controversialist. One so outspoken had enemies but those who survived the noviceship under him retained an undying respect for him.

He showed great self sacrifice when, aged sixty-two, he retired with his novices to Hodder. Here life was anything but comfortable and he retained the post for thirteen years. All those who would later rebuild the English Province passed through his energetic hands. Plowden renewed his simple vows in 1803–4 and was solemnly professed on 13th November 1805. Though devoted to the good Mr Stone, he found him something of a trial. He was happier with the novices and rarely visited Stonyhurst. Each week according to tradition, Plowden as novice-master gave exhortations on the Jesuit rule. So excellent [372]   did these prove that they were still being used at the start of the Second World War. He also wrote out innumerable Sunday sermons. His piety was bluff, vigorous and markedly English; some criticisms were scathing, but filled with common sense. In a way, Plowden's greatest work for the Province was performed in this period. He revived the traditions and spirit well nigh extinct after a gap of thirty years.

At a most delicate period he constructed the future Province in his handling of the novices. His standards were high. Between 1803 and 1830 171 novices were admitted and 62 were dismissed. He recognized and cultivated true virtue when he found it. Peter Kenny, Thomas Glover, Charles Brooke among others, were men whom he groomed for leadership. He left certain notes for Brooke, later Provincial; one was short passage about Lorenzo Ricci, the unfortunate General, copied from a Venetian history. He was a man, it said, of incomparable innocence of manner. He was also timid to excess, incapable of undertaking any business which might require shrewdness, steadiness, or courage. A perfect religious man but a useless superior.

From 1803 to 1814, Napoleon was master of Europe and [373] Pope Pius VII, who started his pontificate powerless, ended it as a prisoner of war. Little or nothing could be done, and ex-Jesuits waited when such waiting might have proved disastrous. The immediate worries of Stonyhurst were that an order still officially suppressed found it difficult to enlist recruits. Vocations were virtually limited to boys at Stonyhurst. The noviciate, grumbled Plowden, is becoming a grammar school. The College staff was made up of secret Jesuits, ex-Jesuits and secular clergy and proved unsuitable for men straight from the noviceship. Plowden sent many of his better students abroad for their seminary training. Others had to be sent abroad because the Vicars Apostolic would only ordain aspirants from Stonyhurst as secular priests.

Gravest problems of all stemmed from the increasing [374] age of the ex-Jesuits. In 1801 the youngest was past fifty-four. Would ex-Jesuit property fall into other hands if the last ex-Jesuit died before official restoration? In America, England and Ireland such pressure grew daily more serious. A great many bishops missed the Society, finding after the revolution how they needed its special skills. Prelates began to speak and write more favourably about the dead Society, indeed to become more Jesuit than the ex-Jesuits themselves. The rapid spread of the Paccanarists would not have been possible but for this. Yet in Spanish Bourbon circles and the Roman curia there was bitter hostility still.

Those who held positions of importance in the Church had absorbed much prejudice in their formative years. In his *Memoirs*, Cardinal Pacca offers a valuable clue to the situation. He tells how he had been taught from his youth to nourish against the Order feelings of aversion and hatred. Pascal's *Provincial Letters* and Arnauld's *Morale Pratique de Jesuite* had been given him and he had not a shadow of a doubt as to their truth and accuracy.

[375]   When such a background is taken into account the long delays seem less excessive, while the decision of Pius VII to restore the Society seems doubly magnanimous. Cardinal Pacca tells us the Pope in the end acted with deliberate haste. As soon as he was released from honourable detention, he decided to finish with the subject for good. The brief *Sollicitudo Omnium Ecclesiarum* was published on 7th August 1814. The Gesù in Rome once more wore all its trappings and some eighty ex-Jesuits stood behind the line of cardinals when the Pope celebrated Mass at the tomb of St Ignatius after which the Brief of Restoration was read aloud. His old friend Plowden sent John Carroll, now Archbishop of Baltimore, the news and he replied with joy on receiving it. The saying of Mass by His Holiness himself on the occasion he found most pleasing, though hardness of style is shown at his remembering the rapine and devastation they had witnessed years before and he regrets Plowden's fears of further opposition in England.

Carroll had hoped in his old age to retire to join the Society
again but he died in Baltimore in 1815.   [376]

The joy of public restoration of the Society felt by many
old ex-Jesuits, never percolated to Stonyhurst. In 1815 Dr
Poynter and the other Vicars Apostolic would not, save
Milner, recognize the Brief. Poynter wrote to Rome to ask
what should be done about it should a hostile English
government object. Cardinal Litta replied that the restora-
tion was only intended where the civil government agreed
to receive it. It was this which enabled Lord Sidmouth's
Tory and bitterly anti-Catholic government to keep the
Gentlemen waiting another thirteen years. The Vicars
Apostolic wanted to do nothing to impede Catholic Emancipation. The Pope and Cardinal Consalvi, rescued from   [377]
Napoleon, were grateful to the English government.
Consalvi had come to London and was a success in high
society. He had a reputation to maintain. Milner,
Plowden's ally, was not wholly acceptable to the Curia
while Plowden himself was irascible and ill-advised.
These admissions sugar the pill, though they do not fully
explain Poynter's behaviour.

The battle of the agents now began. Walsh, Grassi and
the ever competent Thomas Glover on the Jesuit side, who
won the day from the sidelines. Dr Poynter was represented by Msgr Gradwell and the future Dr Wiseman.
Meanwhile the Gentlemen of Stonyhurst watched their
future disappear. Ordination in some parts of England   [378]
was difficult for the young men, and if ordained overseas
they faced a battle for faculties. Memorials, notes, peti-
tions etc. to Rome were questioned and went in vain. The
official excuse for the thirteen-year delay was the Jesuit
threat to Emancipation. But smaller more pressing issues,
the English College in Rome, ex-Jesuit property and
money, the English episcopate's dislike of exempt religious, blended with the hoary dislike of Jesuits.

The controversy was conducted with Regency elegance.
Jesuits no longer charged their adversaries with jealousy,
rebutted by accusations of murder, forgery and theft.

Poynter said he had revered the Society since his youth. Plowden saw his opponents as good men who thought that by destroying Jesuits they were serving God; both sides thought their opponents all powerful. In less frustrating times this long argument might have seemed interesting. Jesuits, questionably suppressed for forty [379] years, saw this further decade of humiliation as intolerable. The Pope had spoken: internationally the Society was restarting. In England, bishops invited the opposition of a Protestant government until finally Leo XII dismissed their scruples with a stroke of his pen.

In the general touchiness, trivial disputes assumed the importance of Ephesus. There was a row at Wigan, Jesuits and seculars competing to finish their chapels first. In the end two parishes rose within a stone's throw while [380] Plowden and Lingard joined in the battle of the books. By 1815, Robert Plowden had built up the parish in Bristol and a South Wales mission, and was much loved after twenty-five years' work among the poor. However he had, in Jesuit circles, long been known for being 'difficult' and he suddenly challenged his bishop's theology on a trivial point. Mr Stone was hesitant, but eventually decided to set off for Bristol, but sent a message back for an assistant. A note from Charles Plowden said that, even if all Stonyhurst should repair to Bristol, the execution would still [380] depend on him.

Good Mr Stone retired to St Helens in 1817. He left behind at Stonyhurst, no walk, no tree, no building to carry the record of his honourable career. One hundred and fifty years later a rector of Stonyhurst, clearing his room unearthed a small, uninspiring book of meditations: the compiler was Marmaduke Stone. Charles Plowden followed Marmaduke Stone. In 1817, Fr Charles was beyond his prime, angry and energetic, his great work for the novices completed but the results still to come. He set out, full of pain and depression to Rome for a Congregation to elect a new General. His last message is in its way tragic: Fr General forbids me to despair. I must obey but I carry a heart and a head almost equally broken. At this point the historian is overwhelmed with sorrow, not certain whether popes, cardinals, Msgr Gradwell, Dr Poynter, had any thought for Charles Plowden's suffering. [381]

Plowden set out from Rome heavy-hearted and died at Jougne on the way home. His companion must have said he had been to Rome to elect a General and Jougne, misunderstanding, provided him with a burial in the village church with full miltary honours proper to a General. No one more deserved it. He died on 13th June 1821, seventy-seven years old, having been some fifty years in the field. His one desire was to train the new generations to the St Omers and Watten ideal. History is cynical, death the only answer. Poynter, Milner, Strickland, Plowden, Carroll had to join Pius VII and Cardinal Consalvi in the land of milk and honey before the tale of the Jesuit suppression ended.

Bishop Baines, agent for Bishop Collinridge, presented a memorandum to Leo XII with Fr Tom Glover, Plowden's novice in the wings. The Pope studied the document, consulted two cardinals who gave their opinions and then with his own hand wrote to the English Vicars Apostolic that, without further scruple, they should recognize the restoration of the Jesuits. The sorrows of good men excepted, the whole situation was vaguely comical. As far as we know, there were no celebrations in England. All but two of the protagonists were dead. Dr Gradwell was busy as a bishop in London, Mr Stone, half-blind at St Helens, was much too holy: no last laugh, we may be certain, played on his cherubic face. [382]

11

The Victorians

[383] The final sections of this survey will differ from the rest. An obvious reason is the dramatic change of status effected by the 1829 Catholic Emancipation Act after which Catholics were free of most civil disabilities, churches could be built in public places, papists became respectable. In 1840 *The Tablet* appeared and seven years later James Burns and a Mr Latimer founded a Catholic publishing house; a last sectarian growl greeted the restoration of the Catholic hierarchy in 1850. Intolerance did not end by act of Parliament; in many ways it grew stronger, and some Catholics were guilty of it.

The heroic achievements of an extraordinary age will lack recognition if we presume at the start of the century that resurgence so clearly visible at the end. The century was halfway through before the revival could be identi-

[384] fied. French emigre priests exiled in England, were appalled at the poverty and backwardness of the English Catholic Church. Nicholas Sewall, from Maryland, Provincial on the death of Charles Plowden in 1821, saw it at its lowest ebb. Sewall, an admirable man, tells us in 1824 that letters to and from Rome were generally opened. The French ambassador agreed to have them sent out in the diplomatic bag.

By mid-century the situation had altered, for by then England had been seen as a genuinely missionary country by Continental Catholics. French and Italian missionaries came, priests and reverend mothers, carrying lace surplices, *Quarant Ore*, and May devotions. Then the moment came when Fr Frederick Faber proudly stalked the Strand in his soutane. The Jesuits, painfully English, may have muttered at recreation but little of their gossip survives. The Jesuit General himself arrived in England in 1848, to find his subjects wearing white chokers, side-whiskers and large leather buttons on heavy brown coats. [385]

In the north, poor Irish immigrants came to escape starvation and settled in the new, ugly industrial towns. They brought ardent faith, a respect for priests, a degrading poverty not of their own making and the concomitant problems of slum dwellers. The English Catholics, mainly rural, faced a new harsh commercial world against which Factory Acts and Trade Unions, Savings Banks, Temperance Guilds, Catholic Young Men's Societies, parish missions and parish schools developed. Priests had not been trained for these conditions. Jesuits were few in number. A Province which had had 300 members in times of persecution, in 1803 could count thirty-three ageing priests and twelve dubious novices.

The long, futile dispute with unfriendly canonists had checked recruitment and played havoc with discipline. Sewall as Provincial initiated a special fund for a new college far from Stonyhurst, to enable the true spirit of the Society to survive. The tardy recognition of the Society [386] meant the plan was ignored. By 1833 there were 112 members of the Province, two-thirds engaged at Stonyhurst, now the centre of the restricted Jesuit world. Outside it there were four Jesuits, or ex-Jesuits, in Preston, four in London; others were scattered across the country in missions of the glorious days. The plans of Richard Blount were still technically in operation but he had known nothing of Irish immigration, or places like St Helens, Widnes or Liverpool. Sewall met old and devoted men, living on their own, and gives us a glimpse of Charles Wright, once procurator at Liège, serving soup to the unemployed near Stonyhurst, and buying cotton for the poor to weave. Sewall is hard pressed to meet his commitments. He takes Wright with him to settle a dispute in Preston, finds Daddy Dunn unbearable, the community at sixes and sevens, leaving him not knowing [387] what to do. Sewall is one of the heroes of a sad period. He was ordained at Liège just before the Suppression, but did not return with his brother to Maryland. He moved to Lancashire in 1774. He, rather than Dunn, was the founder of the Preston mission, one of the best developed in the industrial north. After renewing his vows as a Jesuit in 1803 he had returned to community life and was in turn, rector, novicemaster and Provincial in those depressing days. We last hear of him in a letter of a later Provincial, Richard Norris, who tells of his fast-approaching end, of his being incapable of saying Mass, and only with diffi- culty walking, but is as cheerful as ever and perfectly [387] resigned to God's will.

Sewall and other pioneers did not live to see the harvest they had sown. Some sixty years later a Provincial could say that there are Fathers still alive who joined a Province numbering less than two hundred members; we are now seven hundred. The first radical changes came after 1841, [388] when Randall Lythgoe was appointed Provincial. A Lancashire man and a Plowden novice, he had been twenty-four years in the Order before his final profession in 1836. He completed his studies abroad, in Rome and Paris, and was ordained at Pignarol. He brought to his office an unusual broadness of vision, knowing a wider world than Stonyhurst. Though in seven years he barely had time to initiate his policy of expansion, he may fairly take credit for the Victorian Jesuit parishes, foreign missions and grammar schools.

Though desperately short of men, Lythgoe was prepared to face the needs of the new industrial parishes. He was a missioner in Preston in 1827 a few months before the death of Daddy Dunn. The latter was a nuisance to Plowden and many others, but he faced the problems of the Industrial Revolution fearlessly. As early as 1818 he was planning better schools for poor children, raising funds in unorthodox ways. Charles Plowden saw Dunn as light-headed, predicted there would be a crash at Preston, ridiculed his importuning of ministers in London, the Prince Regent, the Pope. He was a nuisance, but he was right and Bristol, St Helens, Leigh, Pontefract, and Liverpool were soon following his example. From 1833, men were being withdrawn from penal day settlements to man these new parishes The move was unavoidable. Between 1833 and 1901 forty-six missions were handed over and [389] after 1901 so were a number of older large parishes. Lythgoe was not appreciated by Cardinal Manning but was well respected in the Society. He was tall, handsome, magnanimous and cheerful and also had a rare facility for reaching decisions and maintaining them; his reforms covered many fields but he was not spared to see their completion, dying when he was sixty-two.

  As in the days of Persons the English Jesuits gave great attention to the training of their students and novices. A note of urgency is heard after 1840 with the arrival of mature and distinguished converts, many older than the Irishman Tracy Clarke who was novice master, but he matched up to the situation. He was a man of holiness and humour; some of his conferences still survive and make good reading and he held the arduous post for fifteen years from 1845. Clarke it was who decided in 1854 to [390] move the noviceship from Stonyhurst to Beaumont Lodge, once the home of Warren Hastings, and recently presented to the Jesuits. For seven years they were there before they moved to Bessborough Lodge, Roehampton, across Richmond Park, where under Alfred Weld they settled down in 1861 to remain there for a century. As at Watten they taught catechism on Sundays, often enough travelling on foot to Westminster, Wandsworth, Fulham, Mortlake and Richmond. Nearly a century later novices thought little or nothing of walking to Farm Street and back. From 1885 they went in pairs, two weeks at a stretch, to a hostel run by the Little Sisters of the Poor in Vauxhall to make beds and help with the patients.

Jesuits were still viewed with some disfavour, and secrecy and suspicion had an effect on the noviciate, known as Mr Clarke's finishing academy. A clause in the 1829 Emancipation Act forbade the recruitment of new members, to dodge this some boys registered as Jesuits [391] while still at school. As late as 1902 efforts were made to have Jesuits made illegal. Such threats, silly in themselves, were taken seriously. When the novices walked on Wimbledon Common insults were sometimes shouted. Two novices stood on duty by the woodshed on Guy [392] Fawkes night.

The Jesuit noviceship was strict. Hodder drew the comment that it was a farm with a noviciate attached. Here as at Beaumont later, there was bathing and boating, and at the latter they were taught printing on an unambitous press: later in the century such relaxations vanished under Jansenist influence. The novices slept in cubicles, rose at 5 or 5.30 a.m., and devoted much of their time to prayer and work. The Novice Masters were men of some distinction. Morris the historian, Porter future Archbishop of Bombay, Weld and Gallwey were to gain great reputations in other undertakings, but Daniel Considine was most famous as Novice Master and spiritual director.

Many of the novices who carried fish through the streets [393] or made beds at Vauxhall were men of distinction, mostly converts, disciples of Newman, Manning or Pusey, men who had undergone great spiritual crisis. Morris, a Cambridge convert had been a canon of Westminster, secretary to Wiseman and Manning. Coleridge was [393] Newman's friend at Oxford, Albany Christie made the last sad journey with Newman to Littlemore. Hathaway, former Dean of Worcester College Oxford, made his first move to Roehampton when he protested at an anti-Catholic rally in a Leeds hall. Tickell, Walford and Wynn were old Etonians; Hood, Amherst and Hunter successful lawyers, Clarke and Ross rowed in the boat race; Kerr,

Law and Granville Wood had served in the Navy, Kerr distinguishing himself in the Crimean War. Eyre and O'Fallon Pope, both wealthy men, joined Roehampton as secular priests. Joyce had travelled from Harrow to Hong Kong to seek advice from his brother before going over to Rome. The programme was rarely relaxed for these novices. Many of these men had voluntarily lived as austerely, or even more more austerely as Anglicans, Hathaway and Hood for example. Foley told the brothers at Hodder that, while lying in the road after being thrown from a horse, Our Lady had advised him to become a Catholic and Jesuit. Mixed up with these men were boys from Jesuit Colleges: Thurston, Goodier, Plater, Vaughan. John Gerard came to Mr Clarke's Finishing School when he was sixteen. [394]

Many priests now sought admission. Manning was hurt at the decision of William Anderdon, his beloved nephew, to join the Society. Morris was one of the few Jesuits *persona grata* at Westminster. Fr Humphrey, one of Manning's Oblates also entered the noviceship. Newman's relations with Christie, Coleridge and others were friendly, even intimate. Wiseman, as Vicar Apostolic of the London District was quick to recognize the merits of Fr Robert Whitty, an Irishman, once an Oratorian novice, who was to end up as Jesuit Provincial. Whitty had to make decisions in the uproar that followed Wiseman's letter – *From Out the Flaminian Gate* in 1850. At the time of Newman's conversion he was sent by Wiseman to make the Oxford converts feel at home. [395]

St Bueno' s College near St Asaph was built by Lythgoe, to be Liège's counterpart: well nigh inaccessible in his day, it met the need for an unobtrusive spot. In 1848 students and professors settled down happily there. Some Jesuits tackled the Welsh language in order to catechize and they did what they could for the poor Irish immigrants. St Beuno's appears in Jesuit papers to have been unbearably happy. Augustus Law, starving to death, thought of it. Posthumous glory came to it with the discovery of Fr [396]

Gerard Manley Hopkins as one of the poets of the century.
Hopkins was universally loved by his contemporaries. He
wrote his most famous poem at St Beuno's. *The Wreck of the
Deutschland* was first accepted, then rejected by *The Month.*
No great success in the classroom or pulpit, the university
world suited his inclinations, and he achieved his most
useful work in Dublin where he died. In Victorian days
personalities were two a penny: in Jesuit circles Hopkins
[397]   never seemed unique.

Theology at St Beuno's was Thomist, orthodox and dull,
but there were among the professors men of undoubted
scholarship. Tyrrell, John O'Fallon Pope, Charles Plater
and others passed to other work, others gave their lives to
the training of priests. Maher's *Principles of Psychology*
went through nine editions. Joyce, a former Anglican,
lectured for forty years with few interuptions and wrote
on logic, marriage and grace. One learned professor never
wrote a line. Charles Townsend was born in 1854,
educated at Keble College Oxford and became Principal of
the Oxford Mission in Calcutta. Becoming a Jesuit in 1889,
he entered the Belgian novitiate in the hope of returning to
[398]   Calcutta. It was not to be: he went to Beuno's and
remained there till his death in 1945. He mastered innumerable Eastern languages, and had known Newman and
Lewis Carroll in his day. No man of his generation was so
greatly loved. He was ninety-one when he died. Stone
deaf, he enjoyed the Blitz in London in 1940, after which,
perfectly sane, he asked to be sent to a home lest he should
be a nuisance to the Province he loved so well.

The educationalists of Victorian times faced a gigantic
problem; the inability of poor parents to pay for their sons
to stay at school. Catholic parents were among the poorest
and they had no access to philanthropic funds. As late as
1905 in Leeds, only forty-five of the boys met the fee of
£4.10s. a year. The English Jesuits were one of the first in
the field in the sphere of boarding education. The St
[399]   Omers, Bruges, Liège, Stonyhurst combination is very
much older than the majority of English public schools.

Until the 1840s Stonyhurst, along with Ampleforth, Downside and the rest, had educated the old English Catholic clientele. Now a more modern type of education was needed: the problem was to persuade Catholic parents of the value of extra years at school. To his undying credit Lythgoe was one of the first to take the plunge. In 1843 he published a prospectus for a preparatory Classical and Commercial day school in Soho Street, Liverpool. Should parents wish it, French, Latin and Greek will be taught without extra charge. Fees £2. 10s. a quarter. Pens, ink, paper will be provided. School books an extra.

After three discouraging years the number of boys had risen from eleven to twenty-four. A similar initiative in Glasgow in 1859 ran into the same difficulties. After several months the number of boys was fifty. In both [400] Liverpool and Glasgow the Colleges nearly met with disaster. In London three attempts to open Colleges in the 1830s had failed. Of one of them – Lythgoe – had been briefly headmaster. As Provincial from 1841 he, as we [401] have seen, stuck to his aim. He did not live to see the extent of his success. In that year the Province had only 151 members – seventeen brothers, fifty-two students and eighty-two priests – yet by 1905, apart from Stonyhurst, there were Colleges at Mount St Mary's (1842), Liverpool (1843), Glasgow (1859) Beaumont (1861), Preston (1865), Grahamstown (1876), Malta (1877), Georgetown(1880), Wimbledon (1893), Stamford Hill (1894), Bulawayo (1896) and Leeds (1905).

A talent for improvisation guided the Jesuits rather than a long term plan. Mount St Mary's (1842) and Beaumont (1861) underestimated the demand while at Leigh in 1903 Fr Martin opened a school for 100, but it did not survive. Fr Gallwey's in Manchester failed in 1874 because it lacked episcopal approval and the General closed it. Manning blocked a proposal for one in central London. It was as [402] well. Had similar attempts succeeded in Edinburgh, Doncaster, and St Helens they could not have been staffed.

Poverty was the most common mark of these efforts. The Leeds educational authorities in 1909 described the classrooms as in every way inadequate but added that it is remarkable that so much good is done in these buildings. The College in Georgetown found that the salary for a laymaster was double the school's income. At first the Jesuits posted to these Colleges had no teaching experience outside Stonyhurst. The St Omers machine was set in motion in Calcutta, Grahamstown and Malta, not to mention the Cowcaddens and Salisbury Street.

Overextended, everything had to be hit and miss. Jesuits gave their services free but this lead to complaints [403] from Rome at the embarrassment caused to others by this practice. Fr Roothan sent a papal dispensation pointing out that some parents objected to sending their children to free schools. He warned that no pupil should be turned away for lack of money, the legal exaction of fees was strictly forbidden and fees must be spent on the school, not the Jesuits. The pattern varies little in the history of each foundation. The first headmaster and rector was normally an old warrior from Stonyhurst, as were Frs Clough, Seed and Martin. One or two young Jesuits were engaged as masters; some succeeded, some did not. The converts, training complete, found their way into the classroom. Fr Walford, an old Etonian in Liverpool, tried to inject into the boys an appreciation of classical Greek. Fr Hopkins, not successful as a schoolmaster, taught the [404] young Jesuits at Roehampton. Of Eric Burrows, the future Egyptologist, it is recorded that if his class was quiet, it normally meant he had not arrived. One Jesuit of the period, in an uncongenial post, was told by his Provincial that if the Society employed us only in those posts for which we are fit, he would never have been Provincial.

The majority of the new Jesuit schools endured a long period of anxiety and frustration before a natural leader emerged. Thus Father Francis Bacon was sent to Glasgow when the College was on the verge of closing; in a very few years St Aloysius was one of the best schools in the town.

Frs Payne and Welsby had the same success in Preston; Frs Harris and McHale in Liverpool. Progress was seen when a rapid increase in numbers demanded bigger and better buildings, paid for in large measure by the Catholic community itself. Pride in the local Catholic grammar school mounted as the battle against apathy and degradation was won. In Liverpool the College plays and football teams attracted considerable attention. There and in Glasgow the Colleges had the best gymnasium in the town.

The parents' opposition to the Classics lead to the introduction of commercial education. Fr Walford, classicist to [405] the core, found his task unrewarding in northern cities. Only at Stonyhurst, Beaumont and Mount St Mary's did the classical tradition still hold sway. It was also noted that the Jesuits were nearly all good at football, handball, and skating. Stonyhurst never took easily to change yet oddly enough, two of its most distinguished masters and supporters were converts. George Kingdon, educated at [406] St Pauls and convert at Cambridge, showed himself a supporter of the *Ratio Studiorum* and was a dynamic headmaster at Beaumont and Stonyhurst.

Edward Benson, Archbishop of Canterbury, Joseph Lightfoot, Bishop of Durham and Edward Purbrick, rector of Stonyhurst and later Jesuit Provincial, had been school friends and budding theologians in Birmingham as young men. Purbrick abandoned his university career in 1848, and thirty-four years later Benson made the tedious journey to Stonyhurst and the future Archbishop of Canterbury wrote to the future Bishop of Durham and told him that there they sat, before a blazing fire as once they had sat in his study, night after night at school, talking the talk which after all, made him what he is and me what I am. Next morning Benson attended Mass in the boys' chapel, celebrated by Fr Purbrick, and slipped away to say Anglican matins in the church. He greatly enjoyed his visit [407] and went home edified and shocked. When Purbrick later dined at Lambeth on one occasion, a number of pictures fell off the wall.

Purbrick used the patrimony bequested by Fr William Eyre to build the south front of Stonyhurst. Few English Jesuits of modern times earned so warm a reputation. He was chosen by the Jesuit Generals to go as visitor to Canada, and next to act as Provincial of New York. As the decades passed he seemed more pompous, his initials cut in metal over the west wing at Stonyhurst. Stone, Sewall and Plowden left behind no similar memorials. A number of legends reduce him to the stature of a great man of his day. We are told that he issued strict orders about the cut of the vestments to be used in the chapels. Not surprising. He studied in Rome and was continental in taste. Another [408] legend is that he banned the scarlet cassocks designed by the Prince Bishop of Liège. Corny stories should not detract from his outstanding merits. During his reign, Stonyhurst acquired a magnificent Roman chapel, a swimming pool, science laboratories well in advance of most schools, and a lavish auditorium to which ladies might be admitted on Academy days.

[408] No Jesuit entered the Society to become a schoolmaster but in the English Province schools were easily identified with the glory of God. The profound admiration for the Jesuits derived from their self-sacrificing efforts to educate a rising middle class. Frs Walford, Grant, Clough, Seed, Law and other warriors did not work in vain. In the nineteenth century Catholics were barred from universites. The barrier had been constructed by the bishops; Manning in particular judged them dangerous, though a very large number of Jesuits, as converts, were university men. This ban lead to external degrees in London, adopted at Stonyhurst in 1840. The training and education of future masters could not be ignored. Joseph Rickaby, Alban Goodier and Herbert Thurston sat for such degrees. Yet it could be reported that the Oratory School Birmingham had the better teachers. With the universities barred, pupils lacked stimulus. In 1895, Cardinal Vaughan, an alumnus of [409] Stonyhurst, lifted the embargo on Oxford and Cambridge. In April 1896, when they had committed themselves to

property in Oxford, the Jesuits were told that two of the bishops had changed their minds. In September of that year nonetheless, Clarke's Hall (the University would not allow a permanent title) was opened at No. 40 St Giles, to settle in No. 11 in the June of the following year. After so [410] many centuries the Jesuits were anxious and self-conscious, returning to the University from which Campion and Persons had fled. By a freak of history their house stood next to St Johns, Campion's College, with Balliol, Persons' College, just beyond.

It could accomodate few students: five at first, eventually twelve. They were most anxious to know the right people, attend the right lectures, to appear to belong. The first two Masters, Richard Clarke and John O'Fallon Pope, were converts. It is said of Pope that he was a man with such an esteem for punctuality that he would not admit to the refectory a student late for dinner, but would give him ten shillings to dine at the Randolph. Undoubtedly the first Jesuits gained an impressive list of academic successes, perhaps a tribute to the old-time methods in which most of them were trained. In less than twenty years it had credited to it, seven firsts in Greats, three firsts in other final schools, nine firsts in classical moderations; four firsts in mathematical moderations, and the Hertford, Craven and Derby scholarships; and among prizes, the Latin verse, the Gaisford, the Lothian – and the Charles Oldham twice. The [411] greatest of successes was not strictly of Jesuit making, for the young C.C. Martindale, a convert and Harrovian, proved one of the outstanding prizemen of his day.

The vitality of the Catholic community after emancipation seems half miracle half mystery. It would be difficult [411] to find in history a comparable example in which a submerged tenth so quickly raised itself to parity. New religious fashions sometimes register swift success, but here was an ancient faith, for centuries outlawed, but now all of a sudden, able to come to life again. Part of the answer lies in the personality of Newman, a figure unique in English Church history. Newman's very presence

raised timid but talented people above themselves. Even in the Jesuit papers of this period, Newman's presence is felt. With his old friends who were Jesuits – Coleridge, Christie, Whitty, Walford – Newman kept up a casual correspondence, and many letters to other Jesuits have been preserved. Newman apart, honours for this
[412] renascence may not be restricted to a single group. In the educational world, many other communities may claim to have done as much and more than the Jesuits. The Marist brothers were in Glasgow before the Jesuits, while the Xaverian brothers in Preston enjoyed considerable success. Nor dare we omit the teaching sisters – Mercy nuns, Dominicans, Notre Dame, Sacred Heart, Holy Child, Faithful Companions – who did as much for the Catholic revival as any Jesuit or diocesan priests. If the Jesuits merit a meed of praise, this is was not earned by doing more or better, but the speed of their reactions, in itself an impressive act of faith. They started schools without thought of success or much hope of repayment and the same spontaneous enthusiasm carried them to tough and distant mission fields. In 1834, when the number of their priests barely exceeded fifty, the Provincial sent Frs Chadwick and Sumner to Calcutta at the request of Gregory XVI.

Here was a mixed bag; an Irish Jesuit Vicar Apostolic in charge, a community of two French Jesuits, two English, a French brother who had served in Napoleon's armies, and an Italian brother, the excellence of whose macaroni has found a place in history. The College, St Francis Xaviers, had 250 students by 1843. Local ill will and caste troubles caused the English Jesuits to pull out in 1864. The College
[413] survived under Belgian Jesuits. At no time in four hundred years were Jesuit correspondents as informative and interesting as these nineteenth-century missionaries in their letters home. One notes courage in intolerable conditions, a complete lack of adequate preparation, indifference to physical discomfort, and a piety free of cloying conventions. In 1860 the English Jesuits were in many parts of India, North and South America, and the West

Indies. Fr Shea in St Xavier's College Calcutta compares its hall to the Stonyhurst granary. Br Loud in Demarara recalls the milder Lancashire rain.   [414]

The need for missionaries in an expanding world was urgent and Jesuits could be procured easily and without fuss. The Pope, the Prefect of Propaganda, and bishops from the missions simply applied to the General who was moved by the needs of the Church and other considerations, not least the need to stand well with authority. A [415] great many English Jesuits were transplanted without warning. Fr Hopkins, working in a small parish in 1887, was posted to Honduras to be made a bishop in 1899. Fr George Porter wrote in 1886, the Holy Father has named me Archbishop of Bombay and you may imagine my grief and consternation. Among many colourful characters few had a stranger career than Joseph Woollet. Born in Southwark in 1818 and educated at Stonyhurst, he went to St Edmunds Ware, thinking of the priesthood but studied medicine instead at University College. He practised in Leamington Spa, married happily, but after his wife's death in 1846 he entered the noviciate at Hodder, aged twenty-nine. Remarking cheerfully after ordination, in the Provincial's presence, that he would like to serve in the Crimea, his Provincial duly obliged. Back in England in 1856 he worked in Pontefract. There, the builder had removed the scaffolding from the new church before the cross was in position; we are told that Fr Porter climbed the steeple and fixed the cross himself. In 1859 the Provincial sent for him and Woollet jokingly said he he knew he was wanted to go to Demerara, only to get the answer from him that he had never thought of it, but he was just the man for the place. So he went to Georgetown initially as Vicar General, ending up in Kingston Jamaica, his base for thirty-two years. Long letters still survive with details of British ships and sailors and of journeys in Honduras. He returned to die peacefully at Stonyhurst in 1892.   [416]

It was not uncommon for Jesuit missionaries to move from country to country. William Strickland started in

India, went as chaplain on a campaign in Persia, worked in Madurai and returned to England, before moving to Barbados. Augustus Law began his missionary career in Guyana, then after some time in England moved to South Africa. Henry Kerr travelled to India in the suite of the Viceroy, served for a time in Bournemouth, then went to work and die in South Africa. Scandals brought Mgr Talbot, no more a friend of the Jesuits than was Manning, from Rome to study the situation in the West Indies. When such is the situation, he reported, none are so fit to rectify it as the Jesuits. Thus it came about that Fr Etheridge, first rector at Mount St Mary's, was consecrated Bishop of [417] Torona and Vicar Apostolic in Guyana in October 1858. He died in 1878 at seventy years of age and his funeral showed how esteemed he was.

In Guyana we meet Fr Charles Wilson administering a huge parish on one bank of the the Demarara river, and crossing the same river daily to teach fifteen boys in the future grammar school. Fr Cary Elwes, a prolific writer, reached Guyana in 1904; soon after he began one of his great missionary journeys during which he covered 550 miles on foot. Bishop Galton, who once at a fair near Stonyhurst tested his strength and smashed the mechanism, watched one cathedral in Georgetown burn and built another; he also once swam a great cataract on the Essequibo for fun.

[418]   In British Honduras the mission was identified with the brothers Henry, Anselm, Cassian and Silvin Gillet, known as the four Gee Gees. One had a horse called Leo XII. It is not easy to distinguish between the four but from them came a series of entertaining letters. Silvin writes: Morning came Sunday Jan 24th. Mass was said early and Padre Silviano, an Irish schoolmaster, and a green yellow headed parrott, emerged from the Cathedral. Why do I carry a parrott [asks the Padre] ? That's my choir. It sings Santo Dios e Santo Fuerte, Santo Immortal libera nos etcetera, and ends with hip hip hurrah. Henry, after transfer of the mission, moved to South Africa. Silvin reports

that at one mission station he found an equestrian statue of Lord Wolseley on the altar, serving apparently for St James. [418]

Bishop Richards, Vicar Apostolic of the Eastern District of the Cape Colony, visited Rome in 1875. The General pledged him eight missionaries for a College at Grahamstown and a mission in Central Africa. Fr John Lea describes their welcome in Grahamstown. He was to teach [419] at the College with Fr Walter Bridge, of whom it is recorded that, if he placed his biretta on the study-pace desk this was sufficient for the maintenance of discipline.

Augustus Law was not considered fit enough to teach. Instead he practised the concertina and taught himself Zulu with one eye on the mission field. This exceptional man was a close relative of the First Lord of Admiralty, spent most of his time as a midshipman on the China Station reading Catholic books, entered the noviceship in 1854 and was a pioneer on the staff at Glasgow, but after his theology, his health being bad he went to Guyana 1867–71 then to Grahamstown in South Africa. The College opened there in 1876 and three years later the journey to the interior commenced. Ten new missionaries had arrived; one was Br John Hedley, former ship's carpenter and sailmaker from Wapping. Hedley and Law were the only Englishmen in the party of eleven that set out on 17th April 1879. There were four wagons, their wheels six feet in height. The first carried Law and Hedley. They moved at four miles an hour on a four-month trek of 1200 miles, arriving in the kingdom of Lobengula on 17th [420] August 1879. Law proved an excellent letter writer and also kept a log. We have a most powerful account of the customs of King Lobengula's people for whom Law's admiration and affection was great. Law was at his best in a crisis, but he was also impatient and his last expedition into Umizila's kingdom seems foolhardy and unjustified. The wagon had to be abandoned and Law and Hedley staggered into Umizila's kraal, dying of fever and malnutrition. He still kept his log and wrote letters. On 15th

October he said his last Mass, dying on 25th November
[421] aged forty-eight with Hedley beside him. He and Fr Wehl
were rescued in pitiable condition. The noble work that
Law set out to attempt has been obscured by racialism,
colonialism and nationalism. The mission survived,
mainly due to Jesuits of other nationalities, members of
the initial party, and to Frs Weld, Kerr, Prestage, Br
Ashton and so many others who had to begin again more
slowly to complete Law's work. Yet Law provided the
spirit and won great love for Africa by his death. Cardinal
Newman wrote to Law's father after it saying, you have
great troubles on you, but you know better than I do that
they are sure in God's good time to turn to blessings. For
the son whose death may be called a martyrdom, you
cannot grieve too long.

While in the seventeenth century many Jesuits remained
quietly in their hiding places, in the nineteeth century they
did so much and they were so few. In 1880, the year of Law's
death, there were only 457 English Jesuits of whom 82 were
brothers, 168 students and 207 priests. Thus no more than a
handful of men administered nine schools, built up some
thirty large parishes in Britain's cities, and undertook the
labours of two great mission fields. The very scale of the
work attempted by them suggests they undertook too
much. Relaxations and recreations were insufficient, sickness rates high: thirty-three Jesuit students died before
ordination in a period of thirty-three years. At Wigan five
died of typhoid in ten years. Of those who went to Calcutta,
Grahamstown and Guyana, many returned in broken
[422] health. With opportunities so plentiful in an age of expansion, many were indiscreet. While busy furnishing the
house of studies in Oxford, Richard Clarke was twice called
away to give retreats. John Morris gave five eight-day
retreats without a break. Vaughan's capacity for work was
unusual even in old age. In April 1915, when he was sixty-
eight, he spent eight days at Farnborough with Kitchener's
new army, addressing the Catholics of each division, the
boys at the Salesian school and the girls at the new convent

school. On his final day he called on the Empress Eugenie, watched the start of the cross country championships of the 14th Division, chatted to Queen Mary and George V and then made the tedious journey back to London to close a mission in Commercial Road.

Victorians of all denominations were partial to parish missions. The annual mission responded to the spiritual awareness of the age. Poverty, poor housing, illiteracy, lack of alternative recreations, all made the church the gayest of places in the neighbourhood on a mission evening. Many religious congregations specialized in parish missions and the Jesuits were probably third or second best. They were under a considerable disadvantage because few of them were Irish. Frederick Hathaway worked in the sentence, when I was last in Tipperary to produce the desired effect. Fr James Clare was popular because a great many thought he was Irish. The English [423] Jesuits gave as many as thirty missions a year in every part of the country and distinguished priests with many other occupations seem to have abandoned other work for this. Successful missioners need not be scholars or professors. Much turned on elocution and pure oratory. Richard [424] Sumner, so popular in Liverpool, was the master of drama; he would kneel in the aisle in the course of a sermon. Bernard Vaughan was, without doubt, the greatest of the Jesuit missioners. Not a clever or a learned man [425] he had the temperament, the wit, the finesse. His mastery was universal. At Manchester on one occasion the congregation reached 2,000, many of whom had come an hour in advance. After one sermon he was found exhausted, his shirt hanging up to dry.

The various religious congregations had their own traditional approach. For the Jesuits it was the Spiritual Exercises, the Novena in honour of St Francis Xavier, the devotions for a happy death. Jesuits spared no expense in decoration of the altar, and they supported the choir with organ and orchestra. Brother sacristans were an essential part of the Jesuit parish structure. Br William Shaw

reigned for forty-two years in Liverpool. His forty altar
boys were drilled to perfection; his crib at Christmas a
scenic display of great magnificence drew thousands from
every part of town. The faith of the Victorian age may still
be measured by the number of its churches. We forget the
size and number of the problems Catholics faced. Money
was scarce, land hard to obtain as Fr Joseph Johnston the
Provincial showed in his report on the site in Edinburgh in
[426]   1859. Jesuits were not fussy about style, their chief concern
was a devotional air, an unbroken view of the high altar,
and plenty of seats. Buildings were often restricted by lack
of funds, diocesan plans, or limitations of site. In places a
small tin church evolved into a larger temporary structure
[427]   – in Glasgow known as the railway station.

A few of the original churches are still standing, notably
in Preston, St Mary's Friargate. A great many were built in
the old Lancashire district. In the south, Bournemouth, a
late-comer, would one day have five, and Wimbledon
four, Jesuit churches. As has been said, a great many Jesuit
churches were handed to others; parish work was not inte-
gral to our mission and nor had we sufficient men to
manage more than the monster parishes and churches as
in Glasgow, Liverpool and Manchester.

Farm Street, London in its day was surely one of the
best known churches in the English-speaking world.
Mystery surrounds its foundation. It is dedicated to Our
Lady but is known by the back street on which it stands. It
was not a parish church until 1966; in the days of its glory,
there were no fashionable weddings; it had to be content
with elaborate requiems. Until Dr Wiseman came to
London the policy, unofficially, of the Catholic bishops
was to exclude from central London the religious orders,
especially the Jesuits. It would be wrong to imply malevo-
lence. Affection for Jesuits is not a commandment; sincere
men like Manning regarded them as a menace to the
[428]   Church. The Jesuit Superior of the central office in the
twilight period from 1784 could no more than maintain it
in being. In 1822 he had premises in South Moulton St. He

had no church, only sporadic faculties and two attempts to
start a school in Marylebone had failed. In 1834 the Misses
Galiani decided to build a church in St John's Wood and
offered it to the Jesuits. Bishop Griffiths found it against
his conscience to allow this. St John's Wood was dropped
but Gregory XVI permitted the Jesuits to build a church in
central London. A site was acquired in 1844 in Farm Street
but its vagaries meant it did not open until 1849.

The delay enabled the necessary money to be raised,
much of it from friends since St Omers days. The opening
of so large a church in the centre of London caused a stir. [429]
Though it was reckoned that there were no more than
200,000 Catholics in the whole of England, at the time it
was designed to hold 1,000. Cunningly the Fathers
charged a sovereign a ticket on the opening day. Access to
the church was through Farm Street only, then not much
better than a slum. From the first it was a success. On great
occasions admission was by ticket only; the doors opened
one hour in advance. This was the age of the pulpit
dialogues, the three-hour devotions on Good Fridays, of
sermons which made fashionable ladies weep aloud.
When Fr Bernard Vaughan presented his 'Sins of Society'
sermons, Mayfair organized Vaughan lunches and
actresses came to Farm Street to study his oratory. The
Farm Street Jesuits were fusty and their house old-fash-
ioned but behind this incense and old lace their influence
was considerable. The church was by chance opened at a [430]
critical moment in the Oxford movement and the Jesuit
presbytery in Hill Street, and then Mount Street, served as
a clinic for those with Roman tendencies. The architect of
Farm Street, Randall Lythgoe, was compelled to use the
priests available at a meagre period. Fr James Brownbill,
sent to Farm Street before the opening day, was never
regarded in Jesuit circles as bright. A Lancashire man,
born in 1798 when Catholicism was not fashionable, his
elder brother was a Jesuit. Ill health had upset his teaching
career but not the simple fervour of a man with no pretensions and no taste. In old age he used the same meditation

book he had had as a novice. He had two other books on his shelf, his breviary and *The Imitation of Christ*.

He was a simple, average, unaffected man of no great intellectual attainments, who satisfied and more than satisfied the highly educated converts from the established Church. In 1846, dressed as a genial farmer, he received Lady Georgiana Fullerton, granddaughter of the Duke of Devonshire, into the Church. Shane Leslie was patronizing. Serjeant Bellasis, the distinguished lawyer, saw him differently. Cardinal Wiseman gave the latter a note to Fr Brownbill. He found him at home, talked to him for two hours, arranged to come to him for confession and [431] was received on the following day. It was the priest's kind heart and good sense by which he was attracted. Manning had a long talk with Mrs Bellasis and sent her to Fr Brownbill whose kindness she never forgot. Newman himself saw Brownbill in the vital year 1845. Manning said his first Mass, and had a confessional at Farm Street, admitting that he was once attracted to the Jesuits. Much though he disliked the Society later, he would often call at and write to Farm Street. He became the most courteous, powerful and intelligent adversary the English Jesuits ever had.

In a curious way, with his authoritarian approach, his ultramontane views and sincere dislike of those who would not think as he did, Manning showed the very spirit he suspected in Jesuits. One Jesuit alone dared [432] admonish him to his face, his nephew Anderdon, in appearance and character very like his uncle, whose letters to him make amusing reading today. Anderdon and others were not allowed to work in Westminster. They had to content themselves with Southwark, across the river which became known as Botany Bay. Despite the open clash, there is much evidence in surviving Jesuit letters that Manning and many Jesuits admired each other. Not all Jesuits cared for Farm Street. It is rumoured that Fr Hopkins failed there as a preacher, George Tyrell was not happy there and Fr Hathaway preferred to be with the very poor, making his mark at the little Jesuit church on Horseferry Road, in one of the worst slums in London.

Farm Street exercised an unusual influence on the English Jesuits. Busy with their schools, foreign missions, the great northern parishes, they forgot they were supposed to be learned men. One Jesuit would lament that, Fr Waterworth excepted, they had produced no writer of distinction before 1864. It was in that year that Fr [433] Weld as Provincial founded his house of writers at Farm Street. It was hardly to be expected that busy men excluded from universities, who were professional schoolmasters, would achieve great scholarship in the first generation. Alfred Weld himself was typical. He had a science degree, taught the subject at Stonyhurst, and in 1844 became director of the observatory there. Next he was Novice Master, then Provincial, after which he was called to Rome as English assistant to the General and as such he played an important part in Augustus Law's expedition, ending his life as a missionary in South Africa. He also found time to publish his *Suppression of the Society of Jesus in the Portugese Dominions* in 1877. It was extraordinarily learned.

Weld was one of three Jesuits Manning particularly disliked: Randall Lythgoe and Gallwey the others. All three were cradle Catholics, all three from Stonyhurst, men of action and most decided views. Weld's house of writers built up over the years an impressive library and served a number of very able men. In 1865 James Coleridge took over *The Month* in which Herbert Thurston published his first article in 1878. Coleridge, a learned man, was close to Newman since their first days at Oxford. [434] Newman's *Dream of Gerontius* first appeared in *The Month*. He, Coleridge had a quiet sense of humour: in his room he had a box of sermon notes marked 'to be kept dry'. A second learned collaborator on *The Month* staff was also a convert, Sydney Fenn Smith. He came from an evangelical home, his father a parson who taught him Greek, his mother taught him Hebrew. Thurston and Smith would enjoy a considerable reputation for many years. Weld not only established the house of writers but *Letters and Notices*, the Jesuit house journal, and he played a part in encouraging a popular monthly, *The Messenger*, which had a wide circulation. The *Manresa Press*, Roehampton operated by a master printer, Br James Stanley, rivalled the *St Omers Press* in meeting the demand for Catholic literature. It employed sixteen operators until its career was ended by bomb damage in the Second World War.

[435] It would not be fitting to consider in such a survey as this Fr George Tyrell's religious worries which lead to his departure from the Society in 1906. Tyrell, a convert, entered the Society in 1880 and was solemnly professed in 1898. He later admitted he had doubts about his vocation before that and there is evidence that in his last few years in the Society, Bright's disease had been recognized. No English critic of the Society wrote a more penetrating attack than Tyrell, in a long letter to the General. He saw Ignatius as modern and elastic; gradually over the centuries the Jesuits had centralized, crushed all local initiative, turned bishops into mere delegates of the Pope. In a letter of forty pages he devotes less than five lines to the praise of any part of his twenty-six years of Jesuit life. So we have Tyrrell's and Manning's opinion to weigh against the lives of dear old Townie, Br Joseph Hedley or of Fr Reginald Colley, the unhappy Provincial who had to handle the Tyrell affair who was found dead in his bed at [436] Stonyhurst. Tyrell wrote that Colley had been in desire very large, fair and honourable however hampered by the trials of his office and vocation.

Fitting it is to end this Victorian survey on a happier topic and pay final tribute to the Jesuit historians. Weld's efforts to produce learned men turned the attention of the Victorian Jesuits to three particular spheres of work. Coleridge, Thurston and Smith gave their time to *The Month*. Weld himself, with Perry and Carlisle worked in the Stonyhurst observatory, Perry attaining a high reputation as an astronomer. The greater number of Jesuits however gave their skill to recusant history. In Victorian times a number of other Catholic pioneers also gave their attention to this work: Dr Lingard, Richard Simpson, Fr Bridgett. No Jesuit equalled these three. The most learned Jesuit in this field was Joseph Stevenson, who was a novice at Roehampton aged seventy-seven. Much of his life had [437] been spent in the Record Office; he was a pioneer of the Rolls Series and crowned his career with an honorary degree at St Andrews, travelling up to receive it, wearing his biretta at the sturdy age of eighty-six. This old expert gave great assistance to Thurston, Foley and Pollen and did much work in the Province archives and with manuscripts in Belgium. John Morris, Novice Master and Provincial, became interested in historical research at Cambridge as a young man; now in old age he edited many documents in his *Troubles of our Catholic Forefathers* and first gave John Gerard's autobiography to the world. John Pollen, of a younger school, published the first documents of Robert Persons in the Catholic Record Society volumes, while Charles Newdigate spent much time on old recusant books. In one way and another most of these aided Br Foley in preparation of his monumental work. All contributed to *Letters and Notices* and assisted consecutive editors of *The Month*.

The third centenary of Campion's *Brag* was not honoured but on December 1886, with thirty-nine other martyrs, Campion, Briant, Cottam and Woodhouse were beatified.

Epilogue

1900–1939

The story of the English Jesuits must end abruptly at the borders of the modern world. Had there been no European wars, no social and economic revolution to contend with, the Victorian Jesuits in their lace surpluses at Farm Street might have pointed to commensurate results. It was not to be. Victorian security vanished for good. In 1891 the novices from Roehampton, in happy mood, went to Wimbledon Common, as did Kaiser William II, to watch an impressive military display.

In the First World War seventy-nine English Jesuits served as chaplains, of whom five were killed. One writes from Archangel, another from what was once German East Africa, a third from the Dardanelles. Fr Michael King went from Mons to Armistice on active service. Fr Frederick O'Connor, an old sailor, wrote no letters but was [438] sighted bathing in the Sea of Galilee. After 1918 a great many demobilized service men applied to join the Society. In 1914, Stephen Webb had gone to Egypt as a trooper; Leycester King, a cockney, made friends with the French Jesuits in Cairo and was received into the Church there. Between the wars the English Province increased very rapidly in numbers. By 1939 there were 903 of them: 138 [439] brothers, 260 students and 505 priests. On paper at least the English Jesuits of the early twentieth century trained and cherished a number of remarkable men.

Consider three great headmasters; Eric Hanson, Joseph Woodcock, and Francis Grafton who brought three grammar schools, Glasgow, Liverpool and Preston to a high standard of excellence. Hanson had begun at Dulwich College, was an engineer with the General Steam Navigation Company, abandoned this to go to India as an Anglican missionary, took a theological degree at Christ Church Oxford, entered the Church in 1886, taught a year at Downside and then joined the Society. When he went to Glasgow in 1901, his College numbered 170. When he left it it had topped 700 with many of its former students in high positions in city and university. The Scottish educational authorities regarded him as second to none as an educationalist in western Scotland. Woodcock, who had served as a chaplain and spent a week behind enemy lines with no ill results, achieved similar results at Liverpool. Grafton was a chaplain also, and was mentioned in despatches, which puzzled him for he reckoned his only brave act was to ride a horse.

Cuthbert Cary Elwes, the missionary in Guyana, was a [440] great favourite of the Indians of all ages but especially the children. They followed him everywhere and when he was away they longed for his return. An American journalist and photographer, admitting his own dizziness when attempting to photograph a high waterfall, found that Fr Cary had no such problems. The tripod was placed, with one of its three legs resting in a crevice beyond the edge of the cliff. Fr Cary bent over, balancing on one foot, the other waving in thin air above the awful abyss. The least slip would have meant the little man hurtling to an awful death. Fr Elwes suffered greatly in his declining years and returned to England. He remembered nothing of the breakdown that lead to this and he could not understand why he could not return to Guyana, living a sad but active life in England for twenty-two years.

Fr Harry Milner was a missionary of a different type. A late vocation, he began his career as a packer in large Sheffield store, joined the Society in 1927 via Osterley, and

[441] in 1933 responded to Pope Pius XI's appeal for priests to volunteer for the Russian Mission. He was ordained in the Russian rite in 1937 and moved to Estonia in 1939. A practical man, and a tough one, he was among other things an excellent carpenter. When Russia invaded Estonia in 1940 he found himself in Moscow, and travelled through Turkey to Palestine. There he contacted the General who directed him to the Russian College being built in Shanghai. He taught Russian and French, and as a master carpenter his skills were useful. Interned in 1943 in Yang Chu he there acted as chaplain, carpenter and general factotum: he left in 1945 as a virtual skeleton, having existed on little but rice for two years. Returning to Shanghai and his teaching, he had a heart attack on the arrival of the Communist armies, came back to England, and died in Dublin in 1951 aged forty-three.

Though a career like this was exceptionally rich, and there were many others like it, an atmosphere of improvisation pervades the century. There were learned Jesuits, but their work seemed to die with them. Eric Burrows in 1924 accompanied the Oxford-Chicago expedition to Kish and was two years later the cuneiformist expert for Sir Leonard Wooley's expedition to Ur. He was killed in a car accident near Oxford in 1938. Herbert Thurston occupied the same room at Farm Street for thirty-eight years and hundreds of pamphlets, articles and books came from his [442] pen. He admitted he had been going to the British Museum reading room for nearly sixty years. His controversies with Rider Haggard, Conan Doyle, Vincent McNabb and Dr Coulton are best remembered. His greatest achievement was the re-editing, with Donald Attwater, of Butler's *Lives of the Saints*.

John Leycester King went to Prague after ordination in 1930 to study experimental psyschology, at a time when it was still viewed suspiciously. He lectured at Oxford, and conducted research on vitamin deficiences during the Second World War for the Medical Research Council, using Jesuit students as guinea pigs. Alban Goodier was teaching the Jesuit students at Roehampton when ordered to Bombay in 1915, since the German Jesuits there had been interned, and found himself in charge of St Francis Xavier's College. He hoped to return to England in 1919 but his spell had been successful, and he had developed a love of India. Appointed Archbishop of Bombay, he was [443] caught up in the old dispute between the Portugese Primate of Goa and the Church of Bombay because of the former's claim to jurisdiction over all priests ordained in Goa, wherever they lived. It broke Goodier. He resigned in 1926 and, back in England, he found fame as a retreat giver and spiritual writer: his four-volume life of Christ being a best-seller for many years.

John Welsby was a competent schoolmaster first in Malta, later at Preston. He had a reputation as a strict disciplinarian, though his fixity of purpose and devotion to duty was admired. He was also an expert swimmer and [444] diver. Sent to Rome as English assistant in 1923 he became also midweek confessor at the English College in Rome. Praise God Welsby he became known as, and he became an Institution. Many priests in all parts of Britain would admit that the Weller had proved a most potent force in their formative years. His succcess was a surprise since it was at the famous English College in which so many earlier troubles for the English Jesuits had their rise. Aston Chichester's victories were more predictable for he was in every sense a giant of a man. A slow starter in the class- [445] room, he had been sixteen years a Jesuit before he was ordained. His first appointment was as rector of Wimble- don College in 1917; thereafter he was in office for forty-five years. Lord Russell of Killowen was a small boy at Beaumont when he saw him acting as ball boy on the tennis courts. Portly, untidy and with a marked cast in his right eye, his speech nasal, the whole invited mockery but in fact everyone, ecclesiastical, lay, old or young, male or female, Catholic or not, loved him. Chic was fifty when in 1929 he was posted to Rhodesia. In February 1931 Salis- bury was made a vicariate with Chichester consecrated as bishop. He died on the steps of St Peters on his way to attend a session of the Second Vatican Council.

[446]   Resistance to change was one of Tyrell's charges and in the early twentieth century there was something in it. The novices still read Rodriguez in old French; Provincials from 1927–64 had Oxford Classical degrees. Attempts to preserve the old *Ratio Studiorum* were still made. After the move to Heythrop in 1926, a textbook saying that votes for women were against the natural law was still in use. During the crisis days after the fall of France in 1940, Fr Joyce announced to his class a great disaster; he had changed his

[447]   views on the *analogy of attribution* after thirty years.

Farm Street suffered most from the decline of Victorian splendour with the population moving out of central London, though it retained its name and drew enormous crowds on great occasions. This centre of Jesuitry was now preserved by three World War One chaplains. Francis Woodlock was once described as aggressive but engaging; it is no surprise to hear that when he was moved out of a base hospital all the staff gathered to chair him to his car. Devas, peculiarly English, was unsettled as a young Jesuit. The Great War established him: a senior officer in the Dardenelles said the problem with Devas was whether to put him under arrest for insubordination or award him the Victoria Cross. Devas never missed a regimental dinner. Robert Steuart was from the Highlands, and had been a cadet at Woolwich before joining the Society. He disliked the army, was both artist and draughtsman, skilled in Hebrew and absorbed by St John of the Cross. For some fifteen years the combined spirit of these three preserved Farm Street. Woodlock made statements to the press, was cartooned by Low and photgraphed in his Mayfair garden. Devas carried the cares of many hundreds. His one literary attempt, a best selling pamphet, contained the notes he had made as a novice under Daniel Considine. Steuart published a volume of war stories. He was the most delightful of the three, with a touch of Tyrell about him, but his spiritual books rank him with Grou.

Stephen Webb had travelled on business to China, South Africa and Canada before the war; we saw him coping with horses at Suez as a trooper when that war [448] came. Stephen had a one brother a priest, another a monk and a sister a nun, but expressed no beliefs during the war in which he showed distinguished service, being twice awarded the MC. After the war he wished for another one to give him something to do, but failing that, joined the Society and was forty-three when ordained in 1931. He gave his services to the Archdiocese of Birmingham; opening Catholic centres at Charlbury, Bicester, Hook Norton and Woodstock. After a final effort at Kiddington, he moved to Yarmouth to open more Mass Centres. He never noticed where he ate or slept. His trousers, sent to be repaired, had to be recovered, having been sold by accident at a parish jumble sale. Once he took a party of nuns from Yarmouth to Norwich, left them for a moment to purchase petrol and returned to Yarmouth without them. Rather than offend an Oxfordshire housekeeper he buried the suet pudding in the garden. Stephen Webb, unusual, uncanonical, saintly, died at Yarmouth in 1958. Fr Freddie [449] O'Connor, who sailed from the China station to join the Jesuits, taught French at Stonyhurst for some nineteen years. He preached one sermon in these years; his text being, a decade a day keeps the devil away. Six foot two and every inch a sailor even at eighty, he retired to Farm Street, each night reciting the rosary around Grosvenor Square.

This epilogue should end with three Jesuit rebels, if such a word may be used of obedient men. Charles Plater, educated at Stonyhurst, became a Jesuit in 1894, joined the Society, read Classics at Oxford and in the course of his training studied in Belgium, from which he returned to start giving retreats to working men and with a concept of social justice fermenting in his brain. This in its time was revolutionary: it meant extending the Spiritual Exercises of St Ignatius to working men; it worked, a retreat house was opened in Lancashire, and before his untimely death he had sponsored the formation among Catholics devoted to social studies and was planning a workers' College where trade unionists and others could study the basic principles of a just society.

He was much admired by the younger Jesuits, but was thought by some older ones to be dissipating his energies. He was for some time professor at the seminary. He later became superior of the Oxford Hall, finally named Campion Hall, by his intervention; during the First World War he gave his heart to the care of wounded soldiers [450] nursed in Oxford. He enjoyed a great reputation because he was one of the first in England to grasp the meaning of social justice and the rights of the worker in the Catholic world. He acquired his information and inspiration from abroad. The generosity was his own. He went to Malta in 1920 for a rest but could not, he continued to lecture on justice and dropped dead in January 1921 aged forty-six.

Edmund Lester never officially went to school. Born in Clifton in 1866, his mother died when he was a baby and his father, a busy solicitor, had three small children to control. Edmund, being very delicate, was left to do much as he liked. He learned to play the piano and violin and spent his formative years at the theatre. He had no religion but was pious on occasion. Purely by chance a Catholic visitor to their house left behind a copy of Challenor's *Garden of the Soul* which the three children thumbed through, and then paid visits to Catholic churches without permission.

[451]   Edmund became a Catholic to the anger of his father. Accomplished in many ways, he approached the Jesuits with some trepidation, having no Latin and Greek and being told they received only their own students or university men. The Provincial, Edward Purbrick, had no problems in accepting him. John Morris was his novice master and the future moral theologian, Henry Davis, taught him Latin every night. Lester, Victorian and middle class, very kind and talented was something of a social misfit but had a progressive project object in mind; the

vocation of workingmen as priests. In his day Latin was the barrier. Lester began his Jesuit career at Accrington, built up a pious magazine *Stella Maris* to a circulation of 47,000, and organized a team of Fairy Godmothers through whose generosity he opened Campion House, Osterley as a house for late vocations in 1919. Henry Milner, already mentioned, was one of them. In fifty years it trained almost a thousand priests. Lester the master beggar, with a deep humanity and a great love and suspicion of his fellow Jesuits, died at his post.

The critics who thought Charles Plater was wasting his life on social projects nursed a still greater grievance against Cyril Martindale. In addition to First Class Honours in Mods and Greats at Oxford, Martindale won the Hertford Prize and the Craven Scholarship (1903), the Latin and Greek Verse Prize (1904) and was twice runner-up for the Ireland Scholarship. Later he carried off the Derby scholarship and the Ellerton Theological Prize. Yet he was temperamentally unsuited for the donnish atmosphere, so completely committed to the suffering people around him, he could not take his studies seriously. Plater [452] and Martindale sacrificed their academic careers for the hundreds of wounded soldiers nursed in Oxford. Plater died young, Martindale lived to a good old age entirely absorbed with the need to bring the message of the Incarnation to a suffering world. First it was the wounded soldiers, next merchant seamen for whom he founded the Apostleship of the Sea. He sponsored a youth centre in the East End and frequently worked there himself. He wrote endless books and pamphlets on innumerable subjects all with the message of Christian hope. In the days when the BBC was young he broadcast a memorable series of instructions on *What are Saints*.

Martindale was a genius with its faults and dynamism. His full effect on the English Province cannot be judged. Devoted to his order and greatly admired by all, he appreciated Stonyhurst and Farm Street, but he could never limit his vision to so small a world. It was to the credit of his Superiors that they trusted and admired one who could not fit into that world from which most of them had come. It was Tyrell's charge against the Society that it was rigid, protective, negative, guarding from the dangers of the world. Martindale never saw the world as sinful but as suffering. Through a freak of history the Jesuits had been burrowing and building for four centuries. Martindale, like Campion, was motivated entirely by love.

It is a strange experience at the end of a book of these dimensions to wander round the galleries and museums at Stonyhurst; one passes by the graves of Woollet and Shea and of Charles Wright. Among other things there is the cocked hat of Sir Thomas More, the monstrance from Liège, the rope that bound Campion to the hurdle. There too are King James II's holy week book, the jewel case of Queen Christina of Sweden, Archbishop Goodier's mitre, the surplus worn by Lorenzo Ricci, and the old blue uniform once belonging to a college boy. The past four hundred years are still cherished and represented, while ahead one sees no more than a question mark. Since the days of Abraham and Moses, this question mark has enjoyed a deep spiritual importance for those who seek
[453]   the glory of God.

Chronology

1. Foundation of the Society of Jesus 1540 to the Jesuit mission to England 1580

1540 Foundation of the Society of Jesus.
1553 Mary Tudor (1553–1558) fails to impose the old faith.
1556 Death of St Ignatius of Loyola.
1558 Elizabeth I (1558–1603) imposes Protestant settlement.
1562 Fr William Good, in exile, the first English Jesuit priest.
1563 Fr Thomas Derbyshire, also exiled, the second.
1568 William Allen founds Douai College to train diocesan priests to keep the Roman Catholic Church alive in England.
1570 February St Pius V (1566–1572) excommunicates Elizabeth I.
1571 Edmund Campion to Douai.
1573 Campion to Rome and Society of Jesus (Austria). 13th June: martyrdom of Bl Thomas Woodhouse, SJ.
1577 St Cuthbert Mayne, Campion's former pupil, the first seminary priest to be martyred 30th November.
1578 February: Bl John Nelson Martyr.
1579 Fr General Mercurian, SJ accepts Allen's request for English Jesuits' participation in the mission to England.

2. The Jesuit Invasion of 1580 to the accession of James I in 1603

1580   The three Jesuits of 'the Invasion'; Frs Persons, Campion and Br Emerson. Campion writes his *Brag*.

1581   His *Decem Rationes* published. 1st December: SS Edmund Campion and Alexander Briant, with their four companions, Martyrs. Jasper Heywood appointed Superior of the mission.

1582   30th May: Bl Thomas Cottam, Martyr. 1583: Persons directs the English mission.

1584   5th September: Weston and Emerson to England.

1585   January: Fr Heywood banished.

1586   Garnet and Southwell join the mission. Hurleyford Conference at which Vaux organizes safe houses for priests. Weston taken and imprisoned at Wisbech. Garnet takes over. Rapid growth of mission.

1588   Spanish Armada. John Gerard and Edward Oldcorne to England. Persons establishes English College at Valladolid.

1590   Richard Holtby and John Currie arrive in England.

1591   The pursuivants very nearly capture every Jesuit on the mission at Baddesley Clinton.

1593   October: St Omers opens.

1594   October: death of Cardinal Allen. 4th July: Bl John Cornelius, Martyr.

1595   21st February: St Robert Southwell, Martyr. 7th April: St Henry Walpole, Martyr.

1597   October: John Gerard escapes from the Tower.

1598   Appellant controversy.

1600   27th February: Bl Roger Filcock, Martyr.

1601   3rd April: Bl Robert Middleton, Martyr.

1602   20th April: Bl Francis Page, Martyr.

1603   Death of Elizabeth I.

3. James Stuart I (1603–1625)

1604   English Jesuits establish houses at Louvain and Liège.

1605 Gunpowder Plot officially discovered.
1606 2nd March: St Nicholas Owen; 7th April BB Edward Oldcorne and Ralph Ashley, Martyrs. Holtby and Pounde (the latter in jail) the only Jesuits in England.
1608 20th June: St Thomas Garnet, Martyr.
1617 Richard Blount, Superior of the English mission.
1619 Blount made Vice Provincial; organizes mission into colleges.
1622 Consult in London re Procurators meeting Rome.
1623 8th February: English Province established. Richard Blount Provincial.
1625 Death of James I.

4. Charles Stuart I (1625–1649)

1625 King Charles I (1625–1649). William Bishop appointed Vicar Apostolic. Richard Smith succeeds him in the same year.
1628 Attempt to establish a noviceship at Clerkenwell abandoned. Letter on Mary Ward.
1628 28th August: St Edmund Arrowsmith, Martyr.
1629 Charles I dissolves Parliament. 'Eleven years tyranny' begins.
1631 August, Richard Smith retires from England.
1633 English Jesuits, Fr Andrew White, as Superior, sail with Lord Baltimore's expedition to America.
1635 Richard Blount allowed to resign. Fr Henry More Provincial.
1638 Death of Fr Blount.
1639 Fr Edward Knott, Provincial 1639–1646 and 1652–1656.

5. Divine right, Anglican liturgy, Puritanism, Parliamentary rights and Civil War (1642)

1642 January: start of Civil War.
1642 12th December: Bl Thomas Holland, Martyr. Effect of war on St Omers. Some senior boys return to fight.

1644   7th September: Bl Ralph Corby, Martyr.
1645   1st February: St Henry Morse, Martyr.
1649   Execution of Charles I.

6. Cromwell and Commonwealth (1649–1660): Restoration and Charles II (1660–1685)

1650   Cromwell's Interregnum and its consequences.
1651   19th May: Bl Peter Wright, Martyr.
1660   Charles II (1660–1685).
1670   James, Duke of York and heir to the throne, becomes a Roman Catholic.
1676   The Provincial, Fr Thomas Whitbread, warns of rising anti-Catholicism.

7. The fictitious Titus Oates Plot revealed to the Privy Council

1678   September: no plot ever existed. Those condemned to death for taking part in it and executed were innocent.
1679   24th January: Bl William Ireland, Martyr. 20th June: BB John Fenwick, John Gavan, William Harcourt, Anthony Turner, Thomas Whitbread, Martyrs. 22nd July: Bl Philip Evans; 27th August: Bl David Lewis, Martyrs.

8. James II (1685–1688). The 'Glorious Revolution' (1688) and its consequencs for the Catholics in Britain to 1829

1685   Catholics, and Jesuits especially, favoured by James. The Church works openly. The King asks for the Jesuit Fr Edward Petre's attendance at Court. Provincial agrees.
1687   Jesuit School opens in London, near the Savoy. 250 boys, Catholic and non-Catholic. Petre accused unjustly of seeking cardinalate. King seeks repeal of

Penal Laws against Catholics, but is rebuffed.

1688 10th June: Queen bears his son. 30th June: seven Whig and Tory leaders invite William III of Orange to assume the throne. October: the King reverses Catholic policies, but too late. 2nd December: flees the country. The mob turns on Catholics. Jesuits have to hide or flee. Twenty are imprisoned.

1689 Catholics denied civil rights. Restriction on property ownership. Disenfranchized. Careers in politics, armed services, professions closed to them. All existing anti-Catholic legislation reaffirmed.

1693 327 members of Province, 119 in England, 116 of them priests, 155 on the Continent in colleges, another 40 across Europe. St Omers centre of a shrinking Jesuit world.

1700 Fr Henry Humberston, Provincial, sends a description of extreme conditions to Rome: the Church however in rural areas receives much kindnes and tolerance.

1725 Complaints from bishops that St Omers produces too few vocations: impoverishment of heavily penalized Catholic families means fewer pupils. Seriously damaged by fire, the college is rebuilt, thanks to generous benefactors.

1728 The missioners are much appreciated by their flocks and their Protestant friends. Fr Robert Aldred, chaplain at Crosby given a fine ecumenical funeral.

1746 First Catholic chapel built in Liverpool burnt down by mob.

1778 Papist Act. Moderation of property restrictions, protection for priests against common informers.

1780 Anti-Popery Gordon Riots, 4th Jan–6th June nationwide.

1789 Influx of Catholic priests and religious expelled from France.

1791 Relief Act. Freedom of worship. Catholic schools. Some legal and military careers opened to them.

9. The English Jesuits from the suppression of the Society in 1773 to its restoration 1803/14

1773 Clement XIV (1569–1577) suppresses the Society, in response to the demands of the Catholic Bourbon monarchs of Europe, with the Brief *Dominus ac Redemptor* (enacted on 16th August). Papacy the real target: Jesuits, its best defence, have to go. The College at Liège survives. Its story until 1829 is the story of the English Jesuits.

1774 Catherine the Great of Russia insists the six Jesuit houses in her realms and the 201 Jesuits in them should remain.

1776 13th January: Pius VI informally allows them to do so. The English ex-Jesuits meet 29th April. The ex-Provincial Thomas More to administer a central office.

1783 12th March: Pius VI formally approves the survival of the Society in Russia.

1784 July: Gentlemen of Liège meeting at Queens Head Holborn. More resigns. Strickland, President of Liège 1783 offers to run central office too. Accepted. Majority of ex-Jesuits return to their districts in England as diocesans. It is agreed that the mission should keep Liège.

1789 Strickland, having brought order from chaos resigns the Presidency of Liège to give 35 years to planning the Province of the future.

1789 Marmaduke Stone. After teaching the bottom class at Liège for fourteen years is made President of College.

1794 Stone leads exodus from Liège. From Rotterdam to Hull over the Pennines to Stonyhurst. *Ascensio Scholarum* 22nd October. Problems with Dr Gibson, Vicar Apostolic Northern District. Rome gives Stonyhurst status of pontifical seminary.

1801 Visit of the Paccanarists to Stonyhurst. Mutual respect, but no link established.

1803 3rd March: Jesuit General Gruber writes from White Russia naming Mr Stone English Provincial. Informal. No Brief issued but restoration of the Society a fact. Mr Stone takes his final vows and is proclaimed Provincial.

10. Restoration 1814 to Catholic Emancipation 1829

1814 13th August: Brief *Sollicitudo Omnium Eccelsiarum* formally restores the Society. Full recognition of the Province not forthcoming from Vicars Apostolic, apart from Milner. General fear is of threat to Catholic emancipation if granted. 26th September: Charles Plowden starts noviceship at Hodder.

1817 Mr Stone retires. Charles Plowden Provincial.

1818 'Daddy' Dunn at Preston; pioneering response to educational and social needs of industrial areas.

1821 Death of Charles Plowden. Nicholas Sewell Provincial.

1827 Leo XII overrides Vicars Apostolic's scruples. Society in England finally restored.

1829 Catholic Emancipation Act.

11. English Province 1829–1900

1833 There were 112 members. Men being withdrawn from penal times missions to growing cities. By 1901, 46 have been handed over. Opposition to free schools in England lead to Fr Roothan allowing them to be charged according to local custom; no child to be turned away for lack of money, all fees to be spent on school not Society.

1840 *The Tablet* first published.

1841 Randal Lythgoe Provincial.

1842 Mount St Mary's College founded.

1843 Liverpool College.

1848 St Asaph scholasticate; Fr General visits England.

1849 Church of the Immaculate Conception, Farm Street, Mayfair, London.
1856 Fr Woollet, Chaplain in the Crimea and West Indies missioner.
1859 Glasgow College.
1861 Beaumont College. Noviciate to Roehampton.
1864 House of writers, Farm Street.
1865 Preston College.
1875 Fr General pledges eight missionaries for South and Central Africa.
1876 Grahamstown College.
1877 Malta College.
1879 Death of Augustus Law in Central Africa.
1880 Georgetown College.
      457 members of Province: 207 priests, 168 scholastics, 82 brothers. Apart from nine colleges they run thirty large parishes, and missions in South America and Africa.
1886 Campion, Bryant, Cottam and Woodhouse among 39 English martyrs beatified.
1893 Wimbledon College.
1894 Stamford Hill College. Fr Charles Plater comes in contact with Catholic Social Movement in Belgium.
1895 Cardinal Vaughan lifts ban on Oxford and Cambridge. Province opens Clarke's Hall, University of Oxford.
1896 Bulawayo College.

12. Epilogue: 1900–1939

1904 Fr Cary Elwes in Guyana.
1905 Leeds College.
1906 Fr George Tyrell dismissed from the Society.
1914 First World War begins. 79 Jesuits serve as Chaplains, five killed on active service.
1918 Armistice signed.
1919 Fr Goodier, Archbishop of Bombay. Fr Edmund Lester opens Campion House, Osterley for 'late vocations'.

1923 Fr Cary Elwes returns from Guyana.

1926 Fr Burrows, cuneiformist, joins Sir Leonard Wooley's expedition to Ur of the Chaldees. August: opening of the *Collegium Maximum* at Heythrop in Oxfordshire.

1931 Fr Chichester appointed Archbishop of Salisbury, Rhodesia.

1933 Fr Milner responds to appeals for priests to join the Russian Church.

1939 At the outbreak of the Second World War, there were 903 English Jesuits, 138 being Brothers, 260 scholastics, 505 priests.

Index

188   *Index*

Blundell, Joseph 116
Blundell, Nicholas 86–7, 114
Bold, Robert 42–3
Bona Mors Confraternity 108
Bourbon monarchs xiii, 117, 182
Bournemouth 162
Briant, Alexander, Saint 7, 19, 23, 25, 33, 59, 167, 178
Bridge, Walter 159
Bridgett, T. E. 167
British Honduras 158–9
Brooke, Adam 6
Brooke, Charles 139
Brownbill, James 163–4
Browne, William 63
Bruges College 118–19, 122–3, 132
Buckingham, Countess of 78
Buckingham, Duke of 78
Bulawayo College 151, 184
Burns, James 144
Burrows, Eric 152, 170, 185
Butler, John 126–7
Byrd, William 43

Cadwallador, Roger 61, 80
Calcutta College 152
Calcutta mission 156
Calvert, George, Lord Baltimore 70, 71
Cambridge University 184
Campoin, Edmund, Saint 1, 2, 7, 8, 12, 13–15, 16, 17, 18, 19–21, 22, 23, 25, 40, 42, 44, 47, 50, 54, 59, 61, 86, 87, 101, 103, 104, 113, 126, 167, 177, 178, 184
Campion Hall (Oxford) 174
Campion House (Osterley) 175, 184
Carlos, William 89
Carpenter, Peter, Br 87
Carroll, John, Bishop of Baltimore 1, 114, 121, 122, 125, 128, 129, 135, 137, 140, 141
Carroll, Lewis 150

Catherine the Great 129, 182
Catholic Emancipation Act (1829) 3, 144, 183
Catholicae Fidei (1801) 136
Catholicism, revival 155–6
Cecil, John 29, 35
Charles I (King of England) 74, 179
Charles II (King of England) 87, 88, 89, 90, 92–3, 95
Chevremont (Liège College) 107, 108
Chichester, Aston 171–2, 184
Christie, Albany 148, 149
Christie, William 72
Churchill, Winston Spencer, Sir 94
Clare, James 161
Clarendon, Lord Chancellor 89
Clarke, John 114
Clarke, Richard 103, 155, 160
Clarke, Tracy 147, 148
Clement XIV (Pope) xiii, 120, 121, 129, 182
Clerkenwell 66–7, 74, 179
Clifford family 103
Coleridge, James 148, 149, 156, 165, 166
Colley, Reginald 166
Collinridge, Bishop 143
Con, George 80
Consalvi, Cardinal 141
Considine, Daniel 148, 172
Constable family 137
Consult: English Jesuits (24th–26th April 1678) 87, 92–3
Cooke, John, Sir 67
Cooper, John 71
Cooper, Richard 107
Corbie, Henry 118
Corby, Ralph, Martyr 33, 76, 83, 103, 179
Cornelius, John, Martyr 178
Cornwell, John 7, 33, 103

and the Oates plot 92
orthodoxy and loyalty 46–7
reputation 101–5
and social class 102–3
spirituality 104–5
suppression and restoration
     xiii, xv, 98, 117, 120–43,
     182–3
training 50–1, 105–8, 109–10,
     147–8
John XXII (Pope) vii
Johnston, Joseph 162
Jones, Robert 60–1, 80
Joseph II of Austria 120
Joseph, John 87
Joyce, G. H. 149, 150, 172

Kellison, Matthew, Dr 31, 69,
     79–80
Kenny, Peter 139
Kerr, Henry 103, 148, 149, 158,
     160
Keynes, Alexander 94
Keynes, George 67
Keynes, John 87, 97
Kildare, Lady 103
King, John Leycester 168, 170
King, Michael 168
Kingdon, George 153
Knott, Edward 58, 72, 80, 108,
     179
Knowles, John 71
Knox, Ronald 69

Laithwaite, Thomas 58–9
Lamb, Charles 111
Langdale, Thomas 6, 26, 46
Latham, Edward 84
Latimer, Mr (publisher) 144
Laud, William, Archbishop of
     Canterbury 74
Laurenson, John 132
Law, Augustus 149, 154, 158,
     159–60, 165, 184
Lawson, Thomas 118

Layton, Philip 116
Lea, John 159
Lee, Robert 54
Lee, Roger 68
Leeds College 150, 151, 152
Leigh (Lancashire) 147, 151
Leo XII (Pope) 142, 143, 183
Lester, Edmund 104, 174–5
Letters and Notices 3, 166, 167
Lewis, David, Martyr 95, 103, 180
Lewis, Owen, Bishop of Cassano
     32, 33
Liège College 63, 79, 100, 107–8,
     112, 123–4, 126, 127–8, 129,
     132–3, 178, 182
Lightfoot, Joseph (Bishop of
     Durham) 153
Lillie, John 54, 56, 78
Line, Anne, Mrs 50, 54
Line, Francis 107
Lingard, Dr 167
Lister, Thomas 51
Lith, Thomas (lay brother) 5
Little Sisters of the Poor 148
Liverpool, destruction of the first
     Catholic chapel (1746) 115,
     181
Liverpool College 153, 169, 183
Liverpool mission 147
Lob, Emmanuel 106
Loud, Henry 157
Louis XIV (King of France) 100,
     109
Louvain College 63, 79, 178
Lythgoe, Randall 146–7, 149, 151,
     163, 165, 183

Macaulay, Thomas Babington
     Macaulay (Lord) 94, 101
McNabb, Vincent 170
Madrid College 63–4, 72
Malta College 151, 152, 184
Manley Hopkins, Gerard 103,
     111, 150, 152, 164
Manning, Henry Edward,